CELIBATE * * * * WIVES

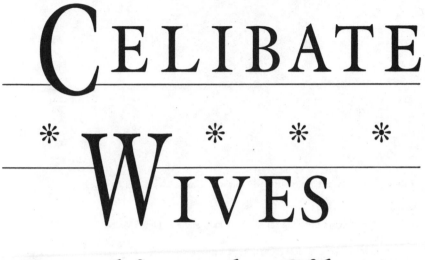

CELIBATE

* * * *

WIVES

Breaking the Silence

JOAN AVNA, M.A.
AND
DIANA WALTZ, M.ED.

Lowell House
LOS ANGELES

Contemporary Books
CHICAGO

Library of Congress Cataloging-in-Publication Data

Avna, Joan.
      Celibate wives : breaking the silence / Joan Avna & Diana Waltz.
         p.   cm.
      Includes bibliographical references and index.
      ISBN 0-929923-99-5
      Sex in marriage—United States. 2. Sexual abstinence—United
States. I. Waltz, Diana. II. Title.
      HQ18.U5A94   1992
      306.73'2—dc20   92-16804
                                                           CIP

Requests for such permissions should be addressed to:
Lowell House
2029 Century Park East, Suite 3290
Los Angeles, CA 90067

PUBLISHER: Jack Artenstein
EXECUTIVE VICE-PRESIDENT: Nick Clemente
VICE-PRESIDENT/EDITOR-IN-CHIEF: Janice Gallagher
DESIGN: Stanley S. Drate/Folio Graphics Co. Inc.

Manufactured in the United States of America

10 9 8 7 6 5 4 3 2 1

AUTHORS' NOTE:

The names and identifying characteristics of all persons described in this book have been changed to protect their privacy. Some stories are composites of several women, but each story is a valuable addition to the overall theme.

We thank each celibate wife who opened her heart and shared her story. Without you this book could never have been written. Each individual story was important, and we will always treasure the time spent with you. Your lives light the way for others to explore options and find their own solutions to a celibate marriage.

AND TO

Patrick Delahunt
who came into our lives
as if by a miracle, who
validated the importance
of our idea, and whose
prodding and encouragement
kept us going that first year.

CONTENTS

ACKNOWLEDGMENTS

This book grew out of the lives, struggles, and hopes of the women who appear (and others who do not appear) in its pages. Lack of space prohibited the use of every woman's story, but each interview added to our knowledge and provided valuable insights that are interspersed throughout the narrative. To all the courageous women whose lives touched ours, our heartfelt thanks.

Our thanks to Martha Millard, our agent, who took a chance on first-time writers and a subject that had not been written about before. Her optimism and enthusiasm for the project and dedication to finding us the perfect editor kept us writing during many months when we felt discouraged.

We are and will remain grateful to our editor extraordinaire, Janice Gallagher, for the opportunity to publish this book. Her expertise, intelligence, vision, and caring influenced us from start to finish. Her insights and support focused, guided, and challenged us to explore ideas and move beyond our original concept for the book.

We thank editorial assistant Bud Sperry for his interest in the subject and his thoughtful input into the work.

JOAN: I thank old friends of the heart who lent their special brands of love and their valuable insights and encouragement at various stages of the writing: Sydelle Golub, Penny Honychurch,

Nettie Isler, Bobbie Lauren, Mary Lil Lee, Ethel Lloyd, Anna Miller, Maureen O'Malley, Sylvia Rothstein, Carmen Sayers, and Dorothy Wilkin.

Deep affection and special thanks to wise mentors and friends: Jeanne Keck, who lent her time so generously and with incredible patience during the earliest stages of this manuscript and who offered intelligent and sensitive appraisal of my efforts; and Carolyn Ring, whose wise counsel, encouragement, and faith in this project never faltered.

My love and thanks to my husband, Eben, and my children and their spouses, Paula, Damon and Karen, David and Sharon, Polly and Manfred, Eben and Sandy, who continue to be big fans and who let me know they thought I was doing something wonderful. Special thanks to Paula, whose research and contacts made my work easier.

DIANA: I thank my family for cheerfully tolerating my long absences while I finished this book in North Carolina and for their encouragement through this three-year project.

My appreciation to special friends who helped boost my morale and sustained me emotionally when publication seemed a distant event: Karen Greer, Marion Otis, Elizabeth Walsh, Rosemary Whalen, and a special thanks to Andrea Mundell, who loaned me her hope and optimism to hang onto when mine seemed to have disappeared.

We thank our North Carolina friends Beverly Boehm, Wanda Haynes, Perien Gray, and Marsha Kummerle for reading parts of the manuscript and for valuable input and enthusiasm for the project.

CELIBATE

WIVES

BREAKING THE SILENCE

"**I**t's time to talk about sex," read the slip of paper drawn from the topic box at Joan's weekly women's support group. Everyone giggled and looked around, whereupon Gail, age 45, haltingly, then with increasing agitation, shared with us the fact that she and her husband had not had sex in four years. Silence followed her revelation. Then the dam burst, and by the end of the evening four of nine women had poured out similar stories of pain, frustration, shame, and anger about their own celibate marriages. There were no dry eyes when we parted that night.

The following evening we (Joan and Diana) met for dinner. We had known each other as therapists and as friends for 12 years, but we had never discussed sex. Over dinner we shared intimate details of our sex lives.

Joan told about extremely unhappy periods of celibacy in her first marriage to a responsible, devoted husband whose sex drive was far less than her own. Although she had been divorced and remarried for many years, talking about it revived old memories of frustration and anger.

Diana confessed that she and her husband had been celibate for four years because of his infidelity. She poured out intimate details of her years of sexual frustration. Several times we found ourselves on the verge of tears as we sat in the restaurant sharing the loneliness and pain we experienced being celibate.

We continued the conversation in Joan's home, and late into the evening we realized how much talking about it helped, how comforting it was to know we were not alone. We talked of the expectations about sex that we had brought to our marriages. We agreed that we had been programmed by our upbringing to expect exciting, satisfying sex with passionate husbands, an expectation reinforced over and over again by the media.

As we talked we acknowledged the disbelief, disappointment, sadness, and despair we had known as celibate wives. We shared the anger and frustration we had experienced in coming to terms with the disappointing reality of sex in our marriages. In discussing the ways in which we each coped with celibacy, we realized we had never seen any books or information on the subject of being married and celibate.

Based on our experiences and those of the women who had shared their celibacy in the women's support group, we wondered if this might be an unspoken fact of life for many other married women. We decided then and there that we would interview women and write a book about this closeted aspect of American sexuality.

To gather information, we placed ads in local and national publications seeking women living in sexless marriages. We were delighted by the response. Most of the respondents, embarrassed by their celibacy, had never shared their secret. They welcomed the opportunity to tell their stories, and *Celibate Wives* was born.

For the purposes of this book we defined a celibate marriage as one in which the couple has periods ranging from several weeks to months or even many years without sexual intercourse. We were amazed to discover that some marriages have been celibate for 5, 10, even 20 years.

We were open about our idea and talked about marriage and celibacy wherever possible. In a dentist's office one of three hygienists told us of her sexless marriage. A woman at another table in a restaurant heard us discussing our project, walked over, introduced herself, and offered to share the story of her 40-year marriage, the last 20 of which have been celibate. Surprisingly, even old friends came forward with their stories.

Women told their friends about the two therapists they knew who were writing a book about celibate wives. We began to receive phone calls from women eager to share their experiences, and in time we interviewed more than 100 women, many face-to-face, and others on the phone.

Although we interviewed a wide variety of women, we do not claim that they are statistically representative of all American celibate wives. They range in age from 29 to 72, with personal incomes from $15,000 to $150,000 annually. They live in all sections of North America, including Canada and the Virgin Islands, and include both conservative and liberal women, high school and university graduates, as well as urbanites and women from the heartland of America. Although most of the women are Caucasian, Black and Asian women are included as well.

During our interviews several characteristics emerged. While many women had a strong sense of hope and a belief that they had the ability to control their lives, many expressed mistaken beliefs that drained their energy and blocked their growth. Common mistaken beliefs included the following:

- Women initially blamed themselves for the problem.
- Women felt it was their responsibility to fix the problem.
- Women believed they had the power to change their husbands.

We were impressed, however, that most of the women we talked with had not taken refuge in drugs, alcohol, and other severely destructive behaviors. While many of them reported verbally abusive husbands, only a few had suffered physical abuse. Many described their husbands as good, stable, responsible men—men these women do not choose to separate from.

We were surprised to discover that there are contented celibate wives out there, too. On June 25, 1990, when we were many months into our book, in a column titled "Sex and Marriage" appearing in the *Palm Beach Post,* Ann Landers responded to a letter from a woman who called herself a contented celibate wife. The writer, in her late fifties, said that she and her husband had given up sex in their forties and were content and happily married. They wondered if they were "oddballs." She asked, "How many other married couples live together happily without sex?" Ms. Landers conducted a poll and informed her readers that she had received over 30,000 pieces of mail on the subject in just two weeks.

Most of the celibate women we interviewed, however, were not in this category. We asked them, "Did you make an effort to revitalize sex in your marriage?" The answer was overwhelmingly, "yes." What emerged is a hard reality of married celibacy: Unless both partners wish to fix the problem and are committed to months or years of effort to revive good sex, it is not fixable. Sex is not a solo act. *Celibate Wives* has no magic formula to "fix" the sex life of a celibate couple.

However, we are hopeful that if you are a woman living in a celibate marriage, this book will:

- offer hope that a solution exists to the problem of living in a sexless marriage
- alert you to the signs of impending celibacy so that you can take prompt action to revitalize your sex life
- relieve the loneliness of the silent sisterhood of celibate wives
- offer specific self-awareness exercises to assist you in evaluating your life

- expose you to a variety of options for staying in your marriage or leaving it
- provide new perspectives to enable you to redefine priorities and invent new life scripts
- encourage you to take control of your life
- empower you to make choices and changes

There are unique circumstances and emotions that go with being married and celibate, especially as celibacy is a totally unanticipated aspect of married life. We are convinced that celibacy in marriage is a well-concealed fact of life in many bedrooms in America today. *Celibate Wives* presents our viewpoints and those of the women we interviewed. We hope that by bringing this taboo subject into the open, we can show our readers how other celibate wives have struggled with their situation.

We also hope that our work will stimulate others to further research celibate marriages. We believe there are two sides to every story, but it remains for other investigators to present the husbands' side. We make no claim to understanding the psychology of celibate husbands or their feelings about celibacy.

Although it may not be initially apparent, we believe there are solutions to the problem of celibacy in marriage. Our intention in writing this book is to help our readers take a more realistic view of marriage and sex, offer new perspectives for celibate wives, and point the way to changes in their lives.

Chapter one shows how a marriage becomes celibate. Among the women we interviewed, nearly 50 percent of their husbands had called a halt to sex. Sometimes it was the wife who said no, for a variety of reasons: infidelity, boredom, loss of respect, alcoholism, illness, spiritual growth, verbal abuse, and incompatible sex drives, to name a few.

Chapter two provides an overview of the grieving process. The demise of sex is the death of a part of yourself. Grieving this loss is essential in order to move on with your life. Women sometimes spend years denying the reality of celibacy in their marriages, venting their anger, bargaining for change, or immobilized by depression.

The focus in chapter three is on the difficulties women have in dealing with anger about their celibacy. It offers concrete suggestions on how to face and express anger constructively in order to move through the grieving process.

Chapter four examines how women cope with their depression, which often overwhelms and immobilizes them as they struggle with their celibacy. We offer suggestions to help women overcome depression in order to make reasoned decisions about whether to stay or to leave their marriages.

In chapter five we explore the possibilities of reviving sex in a celibate marriage. Some women say yes, it can be done. This is especially true in cases of short-term celibacy caused by a change in life circumstances or a traumatic life event. This type of celibacy is often called *inhibited sexual desire,* or ISD, a term that has become the umbrella under which a wide range of sexual problems is classified.

In chapter six we meet women who are deciding to leave their celibate marriages. To the question, "Does celibacy make your life intolerable?" they answer unequivocally, "yes." Each of them has tried a variety of approaches, unsuccessfully, to improve their sex lives. Their challenge has been to find within themselves the resources and self-confidence to make the tough decisions, to take the risks and make the changes that will enable them to strike out on their own.

Can you build a meaningful life in a celibate marriage? Again women say "yes" as they tell their stories in chapter seven.

Their reasons vary, from women who have never had much interest in sex, to others who decide to accept this limitation grudgingly in favor of the benefits of their marriages. Some remain celibate but content, having transcended disappointment and anger and having concluded that sex is not essential for their health or happiness. They direct their sexual energies elsewhere, into family, church, work, or community activities that expand and give meaning to their lives.

We have seen firsthand the affirming and growth-enhancing effects of a self-help group for celibate wives. In chapter eight we offer a step-by-step guide to establishing, conducting, and participating in such a group. As women open themselves to one another, the healing effects of sharing are obvious. If you are living in a celibate marriage, we encourage you to find other celibate wives to provide you with understanding, acceptance, affection, and support as you evaluate your life and work toward making life-affirming decisions.

Active and courageous women have broken their silence, as we have done, to share the stories of their celibate marriages with you. We have done so in the hope that other celibate wives might gain support, derive comfort, muster courage, and learn from our experiences. Many women have molded their lives into successful, happy ones. For any celibate reader, we wish you a positive resolution to your problem. We know that whatever choice you make—to stay or to leave—you, too, can have a meaningful and joyful life.

CHAPTER 1

WHY A MARRIAGE
BECOMES CELIBATE

* JUDY
He'd say, "Don't touch me; get away from me." We went on sleeping in the same bed. There were times when I would reach for him and he would kick my legs hard. I just accepted what he did. I think I felt I didn't deserve better.

* LAURIE
I feel nobody gets a free ride in life. We don't have everything we want, and if sex is what we lose in order for him to stay healthy a few more years, my God, it's a small price to pay.

* DOREEN
When he was picked up for being a Peeping Tom, I felt disgusted, humiliated, and betrayed. I stifled my rage and didn't let him touch me for years.

* ARLENE
Adjusting to a new city, my husband gone a lot, plus the illness of my daughter, overwhelmed me to the point where having sex was the last thing I wanted to do.

* MOLLY
We have a loving relationship without sex. We have a world in common and so much pleasure in being and working together.

The wedding may take place in a church or synagogue. It may be celebrated in an open field, a chapel in the woods, or a gazebo on the beach. The bride pledges "I do" with shining eyes that reflect her dreams of fulfillment and happiness and her expectations that she has found her true love, the man with whom she will share a long and happy life.

If our bride had taken the time before her wedding to list her dreams and expectations, her list might have looked something like this:

I won't be alone anymore.
My husband will be there for me through thick and thin.
We'll grow old together like my grandparents.
We will share every aspect of our lives.
My husband will always take care of me.
We will have great sex, morning, noon, and night.

Our bride clearly expects that sex is necessary for a happy marriage. She has been set up by our culture to consider sex a condition of happiness. In fact, all of us have been conditioned to measure our very worth by how others respond to us sexually and how we respond sexually to others. Novels, magazines, and movies surround and saturate us with the promise of ideal love in marriage, and sex so passionate that we'll explode like fireworks on the Fourth of July.

Every woman in this book expected frequent and fulfilling sex in her marriage. To all of them, the concept of being married and not having sex would have seemed impossible, ludicrous. "Not me," they'd laugh, if they had been confronted with such a possibility on the eve of their wedding. But with the passage of time, a self-assured "Not me" can, all too easily, become an embarrassed and often painful, "Yes, I'm a celibate wife." Which brings us to the question of why: Why does a marriage, which in most cases started out with passion in the bedroom, become sexless?

There are numerous reasons why a marriage may become celibate. Whatever the reason, either the husband or wife may be the naysayer to sex. In our interviews we discovered that in half of the cases the man said no and in the other half the woman called a halt to sex. We also learned that for some women, celibate periods increased over time as the relationship deteriorated, while for others celibacy started abruptly as a result of some devastating revelation. Some marriages moved in and out of periods of celibacy, and some partners went along with sex long after they no longer enjoyed it until one day they said "no more."

Each marriage is unique. Sometimes partners stopped sleeping in the same bed or the same room, but sometimes they continued to sleep huddled in tight and lonely spaces on opposite sides of the same bed. No matter who said no to sex, the very fact of celibacy put an enormous strain on the relationship.

As we interviewed women, a wide and diverse range of reasons why marriages become celibate emerged. For purposes of clarity we have grouped these reasons into categories, as listed below:

1. Mismatched sex drives, one partner having a higher or lower drive than the other, also known as *desire discrepancy disorder* (DDD)

12

2. Infidelity, once or repeated times
3. Emotional, verbal, or physical abuse
4. Illness, whether physical or mental
5. Celibacy freely chosen as a means toward spiritual growth
6. Loss of respect for a spouse
7. Same-sex preference acknowledged
8. Inhibited sexual desire (ISD), loss of interest in sex due to life change or crisis
9. Fear of intimacy
10. Low sex drive shared by both partners

A DISCREPANCY IN DESIRE

Author Joan's first marriage was plagued by the fact that her and her husband's sexual desires were sadly mismatched. Their problem, desire discrepancy disorder, was characterized by Joan's strong sex drive versus her husband Neal's constrained sexuality. This led to periods of celibacy and eventually divorce. She says: "I was not, nor are most women, prepared for a husband with a low sex drive. My upbringing led me to believe that men always wanted sex. 'Women need a reason to have sex; men only need a place,' the joke goes.

"My 28-year-old pragmatic and somewhat pedantic husband Neal had married an inexperienced, very romantic virgin of 18, and I expected him to initiate me into the rites of sex and open up a new world of sexuality for me. Instead, on our wedding night we had a rapid encounter with very little foreplay, and I was left feeling disappointed, lonely, and undesirable.

"I can recall a typical night after about a year of marriage: Neal goes to bed before me, turns on his stomach, while I, perpetually turned on, nag and plead for his attention. What lukewarm sex there was often took place in the process of making up after I had initiated a fight to gain attention. Neal didn't fight—I did that. He reasoned. I think he believed I would 'grow up and settle down' and in time my sexual drive would mellow. It did not. In my day-to-day life I was preoccupied with sex—not enough sex, not good enough sex. I felt deprived, hurt, and frustrated, and I often erupted into anger, while my sense of self-worth as an attractive, desirable woman crumbled.

"Neal was in most ways a very good man and husband. He was a good provider, I could depend on him to be my advocate, he was kind and generous, devoted to his parents, to me and the children. I believe that he loved me, but his natural sexuality was spiritless and restrained, and my requests and then demands for sex appeared excessive to him. I wanted sex daily; he put me off as long as he could. He would have preferred sex every few weeks, which meant that I walked around sexually frustrated and as emotionally volatile as Maggie in Tennessee Williams's play *Cat on a Hot Tin Roof*.

"Whether I was caring for babies, going to college, or packing for yet another move (we made eight in eight years), I continually raged inside, plotted and planned for the next night and the next. Would he be willing? Would I, could I have an orgasm? There were times when my rage and frustration exploded in destructive episodes where I smashed records, kicked the door, or threw dishes. I was stunned and felt ashamed of my behavior when one of my children told me that she felt she was a ship and I was a mine, and she never knew when there would be an explosion.

"The seven-year itch found me staring into my mirror at this unfulfilled, unhappy mother of three feeling that my youth was vanishing. I made a conscious decision to try to solve the problem of my sexuality outside the marriage.

"I rationalized that having an affair would be preferable to the chaos of divorce. I was consumed with the desire to experience sex the way I thought it ought to be—free and open, passionate and exciting, with someone who enjoyed it as much as I did—and I found a partner whose sex drive matched my own. But my heart ruled my head and I was unable to take a detached view of this relationship. The peaks and valleys left me emotionally exhausted and didn't resolve the basic marital discord. I was discomforted to discover that I was really seeking more than sex. I was looking for another man to take care of me and have good sex.

"Several years later I was in despair, ending one relationship and beginning another. I felt chaotic and suicidal. This was no way to live. I did not like my life, yet I was terrified to be on my own. In desperation I entered therapy. I faced the hard fact that Neal's laissez-faire attitude toward my sexual behavior was degrading to me. Sex had become a feast or famine for me. I had no idea how sexual I really was. If I didn't have to fight to get it, would I even want sex every day, once a week, or every two weeks?

"I admitted that Neal had not spent 15 years trying to deprive me sexually, as I had so often accused him. Sex was simply of limited interest to him. I learned that I was not to blame for not being thin enough or attractive enough or smart enough. We were worlds apart sexually and it was no one's fault, but rather a very sad situation for us both, particularly as we had children.

"My therapist held up a mirror through which I came to value my life and worth. He praised my tenacity, courage, and survival skills. I began to acknowledge my strengths and successes, and to credit myself for the tenacity I demonstrated in continuing college in every new town we lived in. I came to recognize I was a great organizer and managed people well.

Counseling fostered my self-confidence and helped me to make the final decision—to get divorced.

"There are times in one's life when everything seems to fall into place, and that was one of those times in mine. I felt good about myself, I had a support system of friends and family, and I was offered my first salaried job. I felt secure enough to ask Neal to move out. The children were unhappy and acting out. Neal never had wanted and still did not want a divorce. My mother agreed with him, and there were periods of intense stress and tension, but I persisted and eventually we were divorced. I knew that I had taken the right step."

When we interviewed Judy, whose story follows, she also spoke of the deterioration of her marriage and the pain and sense of loss she experienced with her husband's sexual rejection. But Judy's loss was compounded by accompanying physical and verbal abuse.

ABUSE BY ANY NAME IS STILL ABUSE

Physical and/or verbal and emotional abuse is a frequent cause of celibacy in marriage. Many of the women we interviewed suffered for years with abusive husbands. Often women do not realize that they are being abused, especially if the abuse takes the form of verbal and emotional attack rather than bodily blows and beatings.

Judy was 29 when she described to us the trauma of her wedding night. "Friends threw us a party after the formal reception," she recounted. "My husband, Tony, never showed up. It got to be three in the morning and I would have left but I didn't know where he was. I was embarrassed out of my mind. When he finally arrived his excuse was that he had to take care of his mother, who was very upset. When we got to the hotel

16

where we were to spend our honeymoon night, damned if that woman wasn't sleeping in our bed right there in the room! I went nuts and ordered her out. Tony just hung back, never said a word. Sex was out of the question that first night of our marriage."

In spite of their rocky start, sex for the first few years was good. Then, as the relationship deteriorated, so did both the quantity and quality of sex. "He traveled a great deal at first," she explained, "and in the beginning it was like a honeymoon on the weekends. When the traveling stopped, the marriage stopped working. The sex became once a week, then less and less, and he started telling me, 'Don't touch me; get away from me; I don't want to be bothered; leave me alone; I'm too tired.' " Many times Tony went so far as to kick her away from him in bed. Judy did not recognize his increasing verbal abuse or even his kicking as real abuse. She only knew she was unhappy and had become fearful and insecure.

Their increasingly infrequent sexual encounters usually lasted less than three minutes and were totally frustrating. "When he felt like it he'd pounce on me," Judy recalled. "I used to watch the clock. Tony would start at 11:02 and by 11:05 it would be over. He wouldn't allow us to have separate beds even though he hardly ever wanted to have sex with me. He lay way over on one side—a big dog could have slept between us."

Judy, as so many other celibate wives have done, shouldered the blame for her increasingly celibate marriage. "It had to be my fault. My mother had been nonaccepting and critical. She used to tell me that I was cold and unaffectionate, that I was really stupid and full of myself. Well, maybe she's right."

Judy began making excuses for her husband's behavior. Perhaps he was working too hard or was depressed, or maybe with his hard-core Baptist background he thought sex was dirty.

After all, his family never touched. "I also suspected Tony might be seeing another woman," Judy said, "and after a while I actually began thinking, he's right, it's me, I don't want sex."

Judy started to believe she didn't deserve any better; she'd have to settle for a sexless lifestyle. When Judy heard her husband denigrating her as her mother had done, it was easy for her to believe him and accept the blame for her deteriorating marriage.

When his kicking left her limping one morning, Judy suggested going to a counselor for help. Tony's response was, "Leave me alone, there's nothing wrong with me." Judy started seeing a counselor herself.

Several months into therapy, Judy was appalled at how easily she had accepted the blame as their sex life took a nose dive, lost all its pleasure, and finally stopped altogether. She had lived on that emotional seesaw shared by women everywhere who are emotionally or physically abused: "It's better, it's worse; it's better, it's worse . . . I give up." As Judy began to gain more self-assurance, she was unwilling to live in her nonnurturing, nonloving marriage. When we met her she had moved out of their home, at which point Tony suddenly came alive with interest, insisting that he loved and needed her.

We asked Judy how she felt about being on her own. "I'm a paralegal, I'm educated, I've supported myself, and yet I'm still afraid to be on my own," she admitted.

Roxanne, a fashion designer with her own income, also found it difficult to name her husband's treatment as abuse and leave her celibate marriage.

We met Roxanne early in our research. She had been married nine years to her third husband, Lennie. Roxanne had married very young and her first marriage had been short-lived. Roxanne and her second husband had been sexually incompatible. She explained, "Both the marriage and the sex were such

18

downers of an experience that I was drawn to Lennie because sex was so great. He was a very good lover, and I think I was too. But in day-to-day living, he was not a loving, caring man and his behavior and language became worse as the years passed."

Early in their relationship, Roxanne realized there was a definite pattern to their interactions. Lennie bounced back and forth between being a tyrant and Mr. Nice Guy. As Roxanne described it, "Lennie probably should have been a king—obviously not a benevolent one. He ruled the roost and would go around bellowing and throwing temper tantrums like a child. When he'd get his way he would calm down. I kept hoping that when he became Mr. Nice Guy, he'd stay that way. Not too bright, was I?"

Roxanne didn't know how to handle these tantrums. "In the beginning I didn't cower, but I became quiet. That's what I do when I'm hurt or angry. Lennie could be very, very brutal—not physically but verbally, and I'm very sensitive. I was afraid of him so I was very careful about what I said. After a while, sex lost its appeal with Lennie. The names he called me offended me and I lost any desire to sleep with him. It was like walking on eggshells all the time."

Roxanne gradually withdrew emotionally and physically from her husband. After being called a bitch, slut, and other particularly vile names, she moved into a separate bedroom. When Lennie barged into her room unannounced and demanded sex, she simply lay there and held her emotional self aloof. Roxanne found it hard to believe he would continue to seek sexual contact. Her husband's temper was so volatile that, distasteful as sex was, Roxanne was afraid to take a stand and refuse him. It was almost eight months before this unpleasant activity stopped. They had been celibate for over a year when we spoke with her.

Roxanne had coped with her celibacy by having an affair. The sex was great. He treated her like a lady. When it ended, by mutual agreement, Roxanne knew she was worth a great deal more than she was getting in her sham of a marriage. When she suspected that Lennie had a lover, she seized the opportunity to file for divorce. She moved out, got a better job, and worked off stress with aerobics three times a week. She enjoys being a swinging single. We asked Roxanne whether she was concerned about AIDS. She shocked us when she replied, "I'd rather die of AIDS than live the rest of my life without sex."*

ROVING HUSBANDS

Author Diana's story is representative of the many women whose marriages are celibate because of marital infidelity.

"Ned and I had been high school sweethearts. I had a short early marriage that ended in divorce after two children. I was soon reunited with Ned, married him, and had two more children.

"During the early years of marriage there were financial struggles, but as Ned's career as a golf pro took off, I felt secure and had no serious complaints about the marriage. Then came that unforgettable night when Ned's infidelity came crashing down on me.

"We had been married eight years, and we'd recently relocated to a suburb of a large city. I was working hard to develop

---

*Many women will be faced with this dilemma if they leave their marriages or seek sex outside their marriages. Unprotected sex can cost you your life. You would be well advised to get up-to-date information and take all the precautions recommended by your local health department, doctor, or the National HIV and AIDS Information Service (1-800-342-2437).

new friends and was entertaining frequently. My husband had a birthday coming up, and I decided that a surprise party would be fun. The kids and I planned the decorations, food, and games, and hid the supplies in the basement.

"The day of Ned's birthday finally arrived. He seemed genuinely surprised and pleased, and the party was a great success. Around midnight people started moving toward the kitchen to leave through the back door, and I went with them to say good-bye. Where was Ned? Talking on the kitchen phone to a woman, apologizing for not being able to see her that night! An old friend realized what was happening and tried to get Ned off the phone, but in his drunken state Ned could not be persuaded to hang up. He made no effort to disguise the conversation. The departing guests understood what was going on and hurried out the door. Ned stayed on the phone, and I fled to our bedroom, where I was racked with sobs and feelings of rage and embarrassment.

"I called a complete halt to sex with Ned. We remained celibate for several weeks. But then I began to feel guilty and was afraid that if I wouldn't have sex with him, that would push him even further into the arms of his lover. I went to the opposite extreme trying to lure him back to the marriage bed for sexual satisfaction. I read books on sex and tried new positions and places to have sex. I redecorated our bedroom with a king-sized bed and bought a sexy fur bedspread. I lost weight, had my hair frosted, kept the house cleaner, fixed more elegant meals, and did everything I could to be the perfect wife.

"During this period Ned's girlfriend started calling the house, and even the children knew what Daddy was doing. I felt totally out of control of my life and terrified of being on my own with four small children. Never once did I say to myself, 'There must be something wrong with him.' I automatically shouldered the blame for the disaster our marriage was becoming.

"Ned portrayed himself as a victim who couldn't control his lover, who was threatening suicide if he left her. We were in counseling where Ned swore he would never see her again and we worked on issues such as disciplining kids, handling finances, and communication. I believed that we were rebuilding our marriage one issue at a time and that we had survived a crisis. Little did I imagine that his infidelity was chronic and would torture me for several years. I eventually called a complete halt to sex. When the children were grown I filed for divorce."

IN SICKNESS AND IN HEALTH

Most marriage ceremonies contain the words, "for better or for worse, in sickness and in health, until death do us part." No couple anticipates illness so devastating that among its crosses to bear is permanent celibacy. However, certain health problems can make it difficult or virtually impossible to have an active sex life, whether because of physical limitations, the effects of medications, or emotional problems resulting from being ill.

Paula and Laurie are examples of how the suffering and anxiety of illness can introduce unwanted celibacy into otherwise contented relationships.

Paula is a 59-year-old woman whose husband was an early victim of the plague of the nineties, AIDS. Horrified at the prospect of contaminating his wife, Marty refused to touch her after being notified that he might have received contaminated blood during surgery. In an instant two perfectly satisfied people were thrown into a nightmare that lasted the remaining 14 months of his life. Paula told us, "He had 13 blood transfusions. He was scared. It was like he had a premonition about getting

AIDS. When he got home from the hospital we stopped having sex. Marty said, 'If I caught anything, I would give it to you.' "

It was a cruel verdict for Paula, who had always been a highly sexual woman. Paula recalled, "I was very secure in my marriage. Sex had been very good. I loved Marty very much and knew he loved me. I trusted and depended on him. Then the illness started. First his nice, curly hair fell out, then he got so tired, then he developed a cough, then he got leukemia, then red spots all over his body, and they all turned purple. I was terrified when he got sick. I took care of him as long as I could."

Celibacy was thrust upon Paula and Marty. At first it was very difficult for her, and she nagged him to have sex using a condom. During those months he would only hold and comfort her, explaining over and over his fears for her health. Sex, Marty felt, was not safe even with condoms. Paula at times could not distinguish whether she raged against his dying or her feelings of deprivation. When the diagnosis had been confirmed, and while he remained functional, they became closer than they had ever been. Eventually Paula sublimated her sexual energy into the long days and nights of caring for him.

It was several years after her husband's death when we interviewed Paula, and she had remained celibate by choice. "I don't feel I would want sex again. I think that I'm finished. When I lost Marty I lost everything, father, lover, husband. He took care of me with gentleness and kindness. But," she added, "I cannot brood on the past. I work for the hospice that helped me care for Marty, and there is a lot of satisfaction for me in that."

Then there is Laurie, age 62, warm and outgoing, who shared with us her sadness about her husband's illness and the resulting loss of sex.

"He was diagnosed with prostate cancer, and the treatment

caused impotence. If he wanted to live, sex is what he had to sacrifice, and since I am his partner that sacrifice was passed on to me. He's in an experimental program, so he may have extra years. But it's always hanging over our heads—he's got cancer.

"It's very hard to watch someone you love die. I don't love him less now that he's sick—if anything, I think I love him more. The times we have together, especially when he's feeling well, are very precious because we know it's not going to last.

"The doctor told us about some device, not an implant, that you inflate and it lasts a half hour. You can have intercourse but not an ejaculation. My husband would do this for me, but right now I don't want that."

Laurie is deeply committed to the marriage and to him. "It's not that I am without any sex. We do touch each other and he will bring me to orgasm, but I feel bad without his enjoying it also, so we don't do it that often. I'm not going to go looking for it elsewhere. I do miss it, but I cannot see myself having an affair. I am more irritable—the word is *uptight*. It's not anyone's fault. I feel nobody gets a free ride in life. We don't have everything we want, and if sex is what we lose in order for him to stay healthy a few more years, my God, it's a small price to pay."

To Live One's Life as a Meditation

Gabrielle Brown, writing in her book, *The New Celibacy*, provides a historical overview of married celibacy through the ages and suggests that, in or out of marriage, celibacy enhances maturity, self-awareness, and spiritual growth.

Nan's choice to be celibate derives from such an ancient tradition, and is rooted in very personal experiences of connection with a higher power. Nan is among a small but growing number of women and men who embrace celibacy for reasons of spiritual growth.

Nan and Evan share a marriage and family therapy practice. Their children are in college. "For years I was a closet spiritual person," Nan revealed. "I read and prayed and remained open." Then began for Nan what could only be described in the words of the mystic St. Theresa of Avila as "an exchange of courtesies between the soul and God."

"I had an experience which changed my life, Nan continued. It began with a series of sleepless nights, yet my energy remained high, and night after night I required less and less sleep. I entered another state of consciousness. In my outer world I marched to the usual drummer. I was a mother, a wife, a counselor, a gardener, but oh, in my inner world it was magnificent. Spontaneously, I entered a period of higher consciousness which lasted for six days. It was incredible. I felt a deep sense of love, and all I wanted to do was to love and serve. Nothing frightened me. I felt protected. I felt in touch with the cosmos. It became the most powerful experience of my life."

Nan believes that she had experienced what that master of the unconscious, Carl G. Jung, described as a "numinous" experience: that which feels holy, sacred, or out of the ordinary. Her question became, "How can I get back to it?"

Nan and Evan shared a companionable and compatible marriage with common interests like gardening and travel. They regarded each other with mutual respect and appreciation. So impressed was Evan by Nan's enthusiasm for her experience, and feeling the need for centering himself, he joined her on her journey and took up meditation. In time he agreed to Nan's request for a celibate lifestyle.

Thus they entered a new stage in their relationship. First came the struggle to quell their sexual desires and their active sex life. Nan described her struggle. "Whenever I had sex with Evan I would be tormented with horrible nightmares, and I interpreted this as a confirmation of my need to be celibate."

In time Nan sublimated her sexuality, but Evan, though he continued to meditate with Nan, felt deprived. Within a year and a half he began to push for sex. Nan despaired, torn between her love for Evan and his demands for sex versus her strong feelings that celibacy was best for her at that time. Eventually Evan gave her an ultimatum: sex or divorce. This precipitated sleepless nights for Nan as she searched her soul for an answer. Abandoning her hard-won celibacy was a wrenching decision. She felt that to do so was to betray her integrity and undermine her spiritual goals. "If I had been widowed I would have remained celibate," she disclosed, "but I love Evan, and the thought of losing him forced me to reevaluate my life path."

Nan made her decision in favor of Evan and the marriage. We had the opportunity to talk with Nan again months after our first interview. She told us that she and Evan had resumed sex, which was pleasant enough, and that she had reconciled her conflict by viewing her whole life as a meditation. Nan felt that she could stay centered and balanced by viewing all aspects of her life—cooking, gardening, work, and even her sex life—in a spiritual context.

WHEN RESPECT FLIES

Respect, as Webster tells us, means "high or special regard." Again and again, the women we interviewed asserted their belief that respect for one's spouse is a crucial ingredient for a successful marriage. Ruth, a realtor in her mid-forties, agreed. "I think respect is the cornerstone of a good relationship, any kind. I don't think I can truly love somebody, adore them, if I don't respect them."

Ruth explained how she and her husband, Danny, had become celibate. "I just lost all respect for him. My successful, hard-working husband turned into a couch potato and he got fat. He refused to work! He just lay around the house all day. I tried to talk to him to find out what was wrong. I tried to get him to go for counseling because I feared he was seriously depressed or going through midlife crisis. I planned family outings to get him off the couch; he usually refused to go. I couldn't believe this was the ambitious man I had so admired when we married."

Ruth became increasingly frustrated and angry at Danny. She was repulsed by his weight, told him so, and threatened him with celibacy if he did not lose weight. Danny ignored her. Finally she moved into another bedroom, cutting him off from sex. This happened two years before we met her. She didn't experience celibacy as a great loss. As she told us, "I don't have very strong sexual needs, though on rare occasions I masturbate. Neither of us was interested in working to make the sex or the relationship come alive again. Danny said he was willing to live in a celibate marriage rather than get divorced. But not me! I'm out of here. He disgusts me. I've lost all respect for him, and though sex may not be the most important thing, I do think it should be part of a healthy marriage."

Ruth has since divorced. She is methodically creating a satisfactory life for herself—which may or may not include a new sexual partner.

Occasionally the "no more sex" decree is precipitated by one dramatic event, a crisis so traumatic that it shatters a woman's respect for her husband, with the result that she cuts him off completely, physically and emotionally. Such is the story of Doreen.

27

In the eighth year of their marriage Doreen's husband, Hank, had been arrested for being a Peeping Tom. "My initial reaction was disbelief," she said. "I was sure they had the wrong man, but when I saw the hangdog expression on Hank's face, I realized it must be true, and I felt as if I had been punched in the stomach and would simply throw up. In that moment I completely turned off to him. In an instant I imagined everyone in town discussing this shocking news. I felt enraged. How could he destroy the lifestyle we'd worked so hard for? And then the depression hit."

We never would have guessed this family secret from looking at Doreen, who at 35 was articulate and self-assured. She and Hank had been childhood sweethearts and had been married 13 years. Doreen was a librarian and mother of three boys. She told us, "Because of connections, charges were never pressed against Hank. I became tight-lipped and stoic. I wouldn't talk about this with anyone. I didn't go to a counselor. I was too proud to let anyone know. Hank tried to explain his behavior several times, but I wouldn't listen. We continued to sleep in the same bed, and the issue lay like a dead weight between us—dead like sex was dead. When he was arrested, I went to bed for a week, then I decided I had to block it all out, including sex, and get myself back to the library—to work.

"That's how it was for five lonely years. I never touched Hank or let him touch me all that time, though as far as I know, he's never done anything like that again. I think Hank is ashamed and he's tried to make it up to us all, with bicycles for the boys, a camper, and vacations to Disney World."

It is sad that Doreen did not reach out for therapy soon after the incident occurred. Talking would have helped her clear up how she felt about the situation. If she could have told her worst feelings to someone who listened and cared, she would have begun to thaw. But for five years Doreen never sought help, never told her family or her pastor or even a friend. A part of her emotional life was frozen in time.

Doreen used so much energy to conceal her secret, she became blocked in many other areas of her life. For five years Doreen suffered from the sin of pride. She walled off her husband and her feelings to the extent that she was no longer available and responsive to anyone, even her children. Her job as librarian was perfect for her. She could hide in the bookstacks and have minimal contact with people at the checkout desk.

Then one of her boys suffered a gash across his forehead and had to have stitches at the emergency room. "I went to pieces," Doreen recounted, "and Hank handled it. I watched the way he acted with our son—gentle and kind and patient, qualities I had loved about him. Something happened and I felt myself softening toward him."

This was the turning point for Doreen and Hank. At long last they began to talk about what had happened and how they felt. They decided to consult an out-of-town therapist. With great effort Hank was able to get in touch with the experiences he had endured during an abusive childhood. With tears in his eyes, Hank said to Doreen, "I am so sorry," and she reached out, touched his hand, and felt the knot of anger in her heart melt. "I forgive you," she replied. That was the beginning of their journey toward what has become a rejuvenated sex life and a more fulfilling marriage.

JUMPING SHIP

"I was 50. I knew I had to do something while I was still young enough to have the energy to contribute to a relationship," Nancy, a 54-year-old teacher, explained.

The relationship Nancy was hoping to invest in was a lesbian one, joyfully entered into, after 35 years, two heterosexual marriages, and three children. Nancy's parents had been alcoholics deemed unfit by the state to raise their children, so Nancy had grown up in institutions, where she became involved with other young women. "My attraction for girls started when I was only seven," Nancy admitted. "I worked hard to convince myself this was a stage and I would outgrow it, even as I became involved with other teenage girls. I married to hide what I was afraid to confront, and to be taken care of financially."

Totally frustrated and unhappy, she kept furiously busy. "But," she recounted, "in the quiet times when I would think about a woman I'd seen or known, my stomach would tighten and my fantasies start.

"I don't hate men," she continued, "I just feel no sense of companionship with them. Heterosexual sex was not nurturing or pleasurable for me." Nancy faked orgasms and dreamed of the day when she would overcome her fears and be her real self. She described her first husband as a romancer of women and her second as self-absorbed. In both marriages she called a halt to sex. Today Nancy lives in a sexually fulfilling relationship with Tina, which gets "more intense and thrilling" all the time. She wishes that she had "come out" earlier but, she explained, "I wouldn't change my life. I needed all those situations to help me mature, but now it is wonderful not living a lie anymore."

A CASE OF INHIBITED SEXUAL DESIRE

Celibacy, for most of us, probably did not crash into our lives like a meteor, as it did for Doreen. It usually insinuates itself into a marriage bit by bit. Celibacy is often directly related to life stresses that strike at the heart of a couple's formerly satisfactory sex life. Relationships suffer, and intimacy and sex may diminish until weeks or months go by without any sex. People come home from a high-stress day on the job exhausted. Relaxing takes priority over affection. An active theatergoer becomes a couch potato, and the phrase "not tonight, dear" can be heard more frequently in bedrooms across the country.

Arlene and her husband had become celibate because they were overwhelmed by life stresses, a situation not uncommon among today's fast-paced, upwardly mobile couples. Arlene's marriage was suffering from one of the many causes of what would be classified today as *inhibited sexual desire* (ISD), a term popularized by the media. Dr. Helen Singer Kaplan, psychotherapist, author, and leading authority on sexual disorders, called wide attention to ISD in her writings. ISD has become an umbrella term covering a variety of sexual problems that may encompass physical, psychological, and situational factors.

The physical causes of ISD can stem from illness, medication, severe depression, impotence, or drugs and alcohol. Psychological causes often masquerade as boredom, indifference, anxiety, anger, avoidance of sexual thoughts and feelings, issues of control and power, fear of intimacy, or misogyny.

Situational ISD traces its roots to life events that cause great distress, such as the loss of a job, a move, illness, work stress and burnout, a death or birth in the family, and much more.

In their comprehensive book *ISD: Inhibited Sexual Desire,* Dr. Jennifer Knopf and Dr. Michael Seiler, researchers and sex therapists, tell us that when a couple comes into therapy, the treatment plan should investigate a variety of factors, including medical history, family of origin, and outside stresses.

Many of the women whose stories fill this book cite reasons for their celibacy that would fall under the ISD umbrella. It is, however, beyond the scope of this book to detail all the varied and complicated aspects of ISD. Books on this subject are referred to in our bibliography.

We met Arlene at a Fourth of July fireworks display on the campus of our university. Was it fated that our lawn chairs lined up next to one another? She seemed high-strung and unduly nervous about her children. We talked about our celibacy project, and as the Roman candles exploded overhead, she told us a little about her life and offered to be interviewed.

The career of Arlene's husband, Larry, had kept them city hopping, and our city was their fourth move in seven years. To add to the stress of adjusting to a new community, Arlene's eight-year-old daughter, Mindy, had been rushed to the hospital with a high fever. Larry had been out of town—again—and Arlene remembered with anguish how the strange new doctor had diagnosed meningitis and told her he thought they'd caught it early, before it went to the brain. Arlene was left reeling with fear and loneliness. The days and nights became a blur of hours spent in a strange hospital in an unfamiliar city with no one nearby whom she could even telephone. By the time Larry came home, Mindy was out of the hospital. In his mind the crisis was over, but not for Arlene.

When we interviewed Arlene, the effects of this trauma were still apparent. Her eyes were dull and tear-filled as she told us, "I was at my wit's end. When Larry reached for me in bed, I couldn't respond. I had nothing to give and I was very angry with him for not being there when we needed him."

Couples suffering from situational inhibited sexual desire find their sex lives profoundly devitalized by the lack of interest of one or both partners. In this case, Arlene lost all interest in sex. She laughed grimly. "Sex? What sex? Who could care about sex? It seems ages since we last made love. Funny, what makes it even crazier is that I used to love sex. Now I'm so depressed I can't think straight."

Larry, exhausted by his new job, paid little attention to Arlene's increasing sense of loneliness and alienation. Arlene expressed strong feelings. "I felt like a displaced person. Eight months and we haven't had sex, that feels strange to me," she explained. "Sex has always been relaxing and a way for me to feel close and intimate with Larry. I just don't feel that way now. Larry annoys me and I feel nervous and irritable. Recently I exploded. I smashed every dish off one cabinet shelf and threw pots at the floor. The kids hid in their bedrooms, and I sat on the kitchen floor in a heap crying. Larry asked if I wanted to get some counseling and I screamed, 'No, I won't go alone—I won't go unless you go too.' "

Larry did agree to go with her for help. We were able to refer them to a therapist. Happily, that was the beginning of the turnaround that revived both their sex life and their relationship.

WHY CAN'T I EVER GET CLOSE TO HIM?

Have you ever complained, "I can't get close to him," or, "Whenever it seems we are getting closer, he pulls away"? If your answer is yes, you may be living with a man who is afraid of intimacy.

Fear of intimacy is a fear we can experience when we feel we may lose someone dear to us, or even lose our very self in being overwhelmed or consumed by our partner. As Dr. Kaplan so succinctly put it in an article for *Redbook* magazine titled, "Why Did My Husband Turn Me Off?": "one partner feels that his 'emotional comfort zone' is being invaded."

Sally, 38, a homemaker and mother of three, began to feel Fred distancing himself from her almost from the beginning of their marriage, though he had been attentive and loving during their courtship.

Sally came from a large, expressive Greek family, very different from Fred's Anglo-Saxon background as an only child raised by his father. The differences in their backgrounds fueled arguments about child rearing, family, money, privacy, even food.

A weekend experience at a marriage encounter with its emphasis on intimate sharing brought them closer, but one week later when Sally asked Fred if they could continue some of the past weekend's discussions, he responded, "What are you talking about? Nothing different happened."

This was the last straw for Sally. Fred's behavior seemed designed to drive her away. She was fed up with having to repeat herself when she spoke to him, though he insisted he didn't hear her. Fred ate in their bed and Sally was tired of sleeping on gritty, crumb-sprinkled sheets next to a man who smelled stale and sweaty after many nights without showering. One day Sally put the kids in the car and went to her parents' home.

The pain of their deteriorating and increasingly sexless relationship had become intolerable to Sally. She returned only after Fred agreed to go to a counselor with her.

Through counseling they began to understand how wounded Fred had been when he was seven and his mother left his father. Fred was afraid that any woman he loved would leave him, and intimacy with Sally was terrifying to him. Therapy helped Fred deal with his painful childhood and taught the couple new ways of communicating that brought them closer, giving them back a satisfying sexual marriage.

COMPANIONSHIP MARRIAGES

Sometimes marriages are companionable even though they are celibate. A couple may have compatible low sex drives, and over time they may engage in sex less and less or lose all interest in it. They may deem other aspects of family life or work more important than sex. We are reminded of Ann Landers' reader "Contented in Montreal," for whom celibacy was acceptable in her marriage.

William J. Lederer and Don D. Jackson, M.D., corroborate this view in their book *The Mirages of Marriage* when they describe the possibility of successful "companionship marriages." They believe that if a couple respect each other as individuals and enjoy each other's company, a celibate marriage can be a happy one. This may seem a shocking idea but is supported by Molly and other women we interviewed.

For Molly and her husband, David, now in their late fifties, sex had never been very important. Molly and David are youthful grandparents, and they are archaeologists, still engrossed in their careers and constantly traveling to work at one dig or another. They hardly give sex a thought. Less sex or no sex was never considered a loss. They have been contentedly celibate for seven years.

"We have a loving relationship without sex. I know couples who claim to have great sex lives, who have nothing else going for them. We have a world in common and so much pleasure in being and working together. I used to wonder if we were abnormal, but now I feel whatever we want is normal and if both of us want the same amount and kind of sex, that's great," Molly explained.

Molly said that sex rather bored them and just naturally diminished. As this was not a problem for either of them, they didn't create one by worrying about it.

There are many spouses who, like Molly and David, share satisfying lives in marriages where sex is of little or no importance. This may be because both partners have mutually compatible low sex drives, or because with time sex has become less and less important to them.

A happy companionship was hard won for Linda and Carl, a professional couple in their mid-forties. Sex had been an important part of their lives until the birth of their children which they had deferred for the first 10 years of their marriage. When Linda chose to stay home with the children, the balance of power shifted. They drifted apart, had disagreements about child rearing, and fought about finances and sex. Carl lost all interest in sex; Linda grew angry, depressed, hostile, and critical. During counseling Carl nodded at the therapist's suggestions, but at home he subverted all agreed-upon behavioral changes.

Linda channeled her energy into education, entering a doctoral program in chemistry. Their lives further diverged and they decided to separate. In therapy, Linda came to terms with their differences. Nine months after separating, Carl, unhappy living alone, began to court Linda. They found that they enjoyed the social time together and could discuss finances and the children without fighting. Carl moved back home and they initially engaged in sex, but it was periodic. Sex eventually ceased, yet their overall relationship has changed and become easier and more companionable. "I love Carl and enjoy his company," Linda explained. "I feel more secure with the dual income and the kids are growing up fast. I've discovered there are things more important than sex."

PLANNING FOR TOMORROW

In this chapter you have learned from the women who bravely told the stories of why their marriages became celibate. You have shared their anguish as they struggled to overcome their plummeting self-esteem, loss of self-confidence, and sexual frustration. Over time they were able to make choices and changes in their lives. We believe that it is possible for you, too, to free yourself from the imprisonment of sexual frustration. Yes, there are solutions to celibate marriages.

Arlene and Doreen, with the full cooperation of their husbands and the help of their therapists, were able to find the solution to their celibacy by making loving sex a part of their marriages again. We will show you how this can be done in chapter five, "Deciding to Work on Your Sex Life."

Roxanne, Judy, Ruth, and author Joan are no longer celibate wives. They built new lives over time, often with the help of counseling, and took the frightening step of divorcing their husbands. In chapter six, "Deciding to Leave," you will learn how women have managed to overcome the difficulties of striking out on their own and thereby found a solution to their celibacy.

Molly, Laurie, and Paula chose to remain married though celibate. Nan would have liked to stay celibate. They made this decision for a wide range of reasons. In chapter seven, "Deciding to Stay," you will learn how women have solved their problem by prioritizing their lives and reaching a peaceful acceptance of celibacy.

A diverse range of marital situations are represented in these pages, yet we will not cover all the possible married-yet-celibate scenarios that cause unhappiness for many couples. The goal of this book is to give you a general overview of celibate marriages, and to broaden your personal perspective about who you are, what you want, and how you want to live, so that you may solve the problem of celibacy in your marriage.

But before you can move on to consider choices for your future lifestyle, you must grieve the loss of the happy marriage you dreamed of as you said "I do" on your wedding day. The loss of sex in your marriage is as much of a loss as the death of a loved one. In chapters two, three, and four you will see how we (the authors) and many other women handled the grieving process, experiencing denial, anger, bargaining, and depression as we struggled to come to terms with our celibate marriages.

If we do our grieving well, we find ourselves optimistic about our lives again. The outcome of good grieving is renewed hope and the ability to put the past behind and move into a happy future.

CHAPTER 2

MOURNING
THE LOSS OF SEX

✴ BARBARA
They say that the wife is the last to know. I had an idea. I had clues.
I chose a way of life—I chose to ignore it.

✴ JOAN
I simmered with anger. I yelled at the kids, I criticized Neal. Nothing
pleased me. I bitched and complained about every place and everything. Sometimes I would lose control and throw things.

✴ DIANA
I was so depressed that doing anything took enormous effort. My
energy level was nil and I lost all interest in hobbies and community
activities.

Celibate wives often describe themselves as overwhelmed with emotions once they face the reality of their sexless marriages. The intensity of their emotions puzzles and frightens these women; they feel out of control and are at a loss to understand what is happening to them. At times they rage with anger, cry in despair, and then feel guilty for losing control. They are often overwhelmed with sadness and self-pity, feeling so depressed that they describe themselves as just crawling through life without the energy for their normal activities.

The celibate wives we interviewed were often surprised when we identified their emotional roller-coaster ride as the normal and necessary process of grieving for the loss of sex in their marriages. It is as necessary to mourn the loss of sex in a marriage as it is to grieve the death of a loved one. It is the initial compulsory step toward healing and being able to create a better, happier future.

In the 1970s Dr. Elisabeth Kübler-Ross introduced the concept of the grief process to our death-denying society. Her research showed that people go through a five-stage process for at least a year and often longer after a loss. She identified these five stages of grieving as denial, anger, bargaining, depression, and acceptance.

You may have heard much about these stages as they apply to grieving the loss of a loved one, but you may not realize that the loss of sex in your life is akin to the loss of a vital part of yourself. It is essential that you grieve that loss as you would any other. Even if you are the partner who has called a halt to sex in an effort to take control over your life, you must still grieve this loss. We've heard women say in denial, "If the kids were grown we'd have a sex life." In expressing their anger they tell us, "I'm enraged that fate has dealt me this blow. I'm entitled to sex in my marriage." Often women bargain with God or with themselves, and we frequently hear, "If I lose 25 pounds he'll want to have sex with me again." Women deplore the fact that they are so depressed they can barely function in their day-to-day activities; they complain, "I am totally without energy or motivation. I seem to stumble through my days." They reach acceptance when they say, "I know I can't change my husband, so I'm trying to build positive things into my life and make new friends."

This need to grieve cannot be glossed over or minimized. In grieving the loss of your sex life you will pass through these five stages but not necessarily in a fixed order. Until you come to terms with the loss of sex in your marriage and grieve what might have been, you cannot make a considered decision about what to do with the rest of your life.

No one says it more succinctly than Judith Tatelbaum in her sensitive self-help book, *The Courage to Grieve*. She helps us see that endings lead to new beginnings. Through the grief experience she credits the human spirit with the resilience and courage to complete the mourning process and get on with the business of living. The mourning period, she tells us, "is a time of convalescence," and she emphasizes the need for us to face our loss and all the feelings it evokes in order to heal the "great wound" created by the loss.

We mourn the loss of sex in our marriages—the physical closeness, the release of orgasm, and the emotional satisfaction of feeling intimate. As part of the process we mourn the loss of our roles as lover, playmate, and sexy lady if we choose not to seek sex outside our marriages. Celibacy became a part of

Diana's life just when she felt sex and her life with Ned might be better. Her sense of loss led her into a pit of depression.

"I was in no way ready to give up sex for the rest of my life. I had reached the stage where my children were growing up and often out of the house in the evening and we finally had some peace and privacy at home. I looked forward to candlelight dinners, shared baths, the freedom to chase each other around naked and have sex anywhere we chose. At a time when my expectations for sex were increasing, our sex life was crushed by the revelations of my husband's continuing infidelities. I called a halt to all sex between us. I cried, I raged, I questioned how life could be so cruel and went into a deep depression. I needed to grieve my lost sex life, my crumbling marriage, and all the dreams I had for a loving, affectionate relationship with my husband."

What does it mean to grieve or to do our "grief work"? It means getting our feelings up and out, expressing them verbally and often physically as we deal with the dead parts of our marriages. It is not enough just to say, for instance, "I'm really angry at Bob for forcing me into this role of celibate wife." You need to *feel* the anger, experience it in your body, and express it in your tone of voice, facial expressions, and body language. Picture the difference between a woman sitting primly in her chair with a wistful look on her face saying in a soft voice, "I'm so angry," and another woman who jumps from her chair, face flushed, fists clenched, yelling, "I'm so damned angry with him—sometimes I hate him!" Obviously the second woman is experiencing and expressing the emotions that go with being very angry.

Many celibate wives have difficulty directly expressing so-called negative emotions. They don't allow people to know their hurts or fears. They deny their anger or depression, and they put on a happy face for the world to see. When their feelings begin to surface they are often afraid to experience them; they feel as if they are losing control and quickly turn to doing other things. Once again they have cut themselves off from their emotions and have postponed the necessary grieving for their lost sex lives.

If, as you read this chapter, you feel sad about what has happened to your marriage or you begin to feel anger welling up from deep inside, it may be helpful to stop and give yourself time to experience these emotions. You may want to sit quietly alone and allow yourself to feel the feelings. It's okay to feel bad—that is the way we grieve.

The stages of grief, which we will look at in this chapter, may be experienced all at once or at different times and not necessarily in order. You may find yourself moving from bargaining to depression, to anger, to denial, to anger, back to bargaining, and so on. Seems endless, doesn't it? We assure you the grief will end.

DENIAL—IF I DON'T SEE I WON'T BELIEVE

Denial helps you postpone the truth about your life. It can be a protective device, a survival technique to keep you from dealing with things that you are not emotionally capable of handling at the time. You should not allow anyone (no matter how well intentioned) to rip away your defenses and force you into confronting your situation before you are ready. If a friend, relative, or counselor, trying to be helpful, starts to force you to deal with your celibate marriage, end the conversation and remove yourself from the scene. You have the right and privilege of setting your own pace when you are confronting your marital problems.

Usually denial crumbles piece by piece. At first you cling to the idea that celibacy is only temporary and your sex life will improve as circumstances change. Then you may recognize that your marriage is celibate but you are hopeful that a miracle will occur and you will be able to return to better days. You may grasp at any little straw—a smile or gesture of friendliness from your spouse—hoping that this is the beginning of the road back to sexual intimacy. But these gestures may appear less and less frequently, until one day you are crushed when you realize that sex will no longer be a part of your marriage.

Barbara, at 65, is still positive and energetic. During her 30-year marriage she worked with her husband, Sol, in his business and presented to the world the image of a perfectly groomed, optimistic, and happily married woman. Her sunny exterior masked the truth of her life, for Sol's sexual disinterest in her began on their honeymoon. "I was a virgin and shy, so when we had no sex on our honeymoon I excused him, telling myself he was young and inexperienced also."

Barbara spoke in a detached manner about Sol's infidelity and their seven years of celibacy, as if relating someone else's story. Even when his unfaithfulness was thrown in her face she preferred to look the other way, for Sol was, as she said, "number one in my life." Her denial protected her from having to confront him, from having to deal with what was to her the shattering disaster of divorce. As she declared, "I loved him completely. When he walked into a room it lit up for me." Today Barbara admits, "My refusal to deal with the truth held me back from becoming a person."

Barbara saw life as she chose to see it, and for her, focusing on its best and brightest aspects was imperative. Short of stature and often overweight, she preferred to visualize herself in her mirror as tall and thin. She dieted strenuously in an effort to please and attract Sol, long after he had lost interest in her.

Throughout this chapter we shall hear how Barbara coped with the stages of grieving. Over the years Barbara's sex life with

Sol was disappointing, and as it became less and less frequent and they finally became celibate, she continued to excuse his rejection of her by blaming her weight, which yo-yoed up and down, and later the medication he took for a heart condition.

Avoidance and denial became a way of life for Barbara. She considered herself "very weak." Her philosophy, she declared, was, "When things happen to me, if I ignore them they'll go away. I did not confront people; my way was to avoid them." And Barbara avoided not only people but issues as well.

Years later, when Sol was actively engaged in a long-term affair, Barbara continued to deny the truth about their marriage. She told us, "I didn't believe that the man I married, that basically decent man, could do this to me."

Barbara admitted that there had always been clues to Sol's infidelity, and she had declined to acknowledge them. "I avoided the truth. At one point his technique in bed changed—he became very knowledgeable. I suspected! There were other clues. I played bridge with the girls every Wednesday and he would come home at midnight. There were other times when he told me he was working late. I would call his office and he wasn't there. I think I knew and I didn't know. I didn't want to know, though deep inside I always knew."

Barbara developed a pattern designed to deny her own sexuality. She would putter late at night in the kitchen and then stretch out on the living room couch with a book until 3 or 4 A.M. There were long stretches of celibacy, yet even with the loneliness, the anger, and the hurt she felt when she was forced to face the fact that Sol had a lover, Barbara again chose to look the other way. She insisted, "I saw myself as an extension of Sol. He was first in my life and I continued to cater to him."

You may be surprised by the depth of Barbara's denial and wonder whether you are facing the truth about the celibacy in your own life. If so, you may find it useful to work through the following exercise. Get a notebook and set it aside for the purpose of keeping it as a journal, a record of the various insights you might gain as you do the exercises offered throughout this book.

It is easy to forget exactly what happened and how you really felt yesterday—or even earlier today. The time you commit to writing in your journal provides a quiet, private space in which to gather and examine your thoughts and delve into your deepest feelings, dreams, and hopes. It is the uncensored history of who you are and what you want.

This exercise may help you to determine if you are denying the reality of the situation. It may help you to see the ways you use denial to shut off thinking about your celibacy. Whether you decide you are ready to deal with this reality or choose to put it off for a while, it is better for you to understand where you are in the grieving process.

EXERCISE

How Deep Is My Denial?

Have you been denying the truth about your marriage or the depth of your pain? Number a page in your journal from 1 to 8 and write True next to those statements that describe you:

1. I really try hard not to focus on the bad things in my marriage, but try to find positive aspects instead.
2. I find that if I keep busy enough I don't have time to think much about my marriage.
3. My marriage really isn't so bad—I know other women who are much worse off.

4. My husband really means well, he just can't always control what he says and does.
5. I often find myself making excuses for my husband's behavior to our children, family, or friends.
6. When we have a fight I go out and buy a new dress or something for the house. I always feel better.
7. When I go out I always try to be nicely dressed, wear attractive makeup, and have a smile on my face no matter how bad I may feel.
8. I know that our problems are only temporary. We would never be the type of couple who ends up in divorce court.

Barbara had engaged in many of the behaviors listed above to sustain her denial. She kept extremely busy with her work, family, and social activities. Well-groomed, she presented to the world a smiling face and an upbeat attitude. She held fast to the idea that she was married to Sol for good, that his sense of responsibility and love for the children would prevent him from ever walking out on her.

Diana, like Barbara, denied the reality of her marital problems as her life moved at whirlwind speed. "I realize now I avoided thinking about my deteriorating marriage by keeping very busy. My four children had busy schedules, and I felt like a taxi driver chauffeuring them. I drove a car pool, volunteered as a Brownie leader, taught Sunday school, and did social work for our church. My many painting, wallpapering, and furniture refinishing projects filled my evenings, and by bedtime I was too tired to toss and turn fretting about my marriage. I found that the harder and faster I ran, the less time and energy I had to spend thinking about my marriage or my sex life. I really ran myself ragged."

If, after considering the statements above, you recognize that you are denying the reality of your celibate marriage, it is up to you to decide if you are ready to confront your situation. If so, begin to think about how sex died in your marriage. Take it slowly. Understanding usually comes in waves as we are able to cope with it. You may feel, as many women in celibate marriages do, embarrassed or ashamed to admit that sex, which you may consider a natural and vital part of marriage, is not part of yours.

However, when you feel ready, we suggest that you choose a trusted friend or therapist to whom you will reveal your secret celibacy. You may find that talking about it is easier than you imagined it would be. Most of the women we interviewed found it easy to tell their stories once they got started. By breaking the silence about celibacy, you take your first step toward healing and building a better future for yourself.

ANGER—MORE THAN I CAN BEAR

When we are angry, our life energy is diverted away from the positive activities of growth and happiness and is often squandered in struggling to change our husbands in hopes of fixing our unhappy marriages. It cannot be said too often: *We only have the power to change ourselves.*

Anger awaits its turn eagerly at the heels of denial. Once you accept the reality of your situation as a celibate wife, you may be flooded with anger, often bordering on rage. You may find yourself angry at your husband, at yourself, at God, at the world in general, or at anyone who chances to cross your path on a particularly bad day.

Many celibate wives are surprised and frightened by the depth and intensity of their anger. You may be among those who scream and yell, throw things, slam doors, smash dishes, lash out at your children, or kick the cat. You may feel embarrassed or guilty about your behavior, and say in a stunned voice, "I can't believe I did that."

Joan recalls a time when she raved, her anger out of control. "I was raised in a passionate, volatile, extended family whose members were in business together. They didn't discuss—they argued and shouted, and later they sat and ate and laughed together. I was able to express anger and didn't think it meant damaging the relationship permanently. I too could fly into a rage and once it was over, make up and forget it. Still, the anger I felt about being deprived of sex seethed and festered in me for years.

"A particularly angry scene took place when Neal and I were married about two years. One night, after cajoling and begging for sex night after night for a week or more, I started a blistering fight. Before long I was so out of control I started throwing things, and then I smashed an entire record collection. As I sat on the living room floor picking up the small black pieces, I remember finding the halves of one record and hugging them to my breast, rocking back and forth crying."

Of course you are angry if you are a celibate wife! For whatever reason, you have been deprived of one of the most basic pleasures of life, good sex. You may find that, just as the women we interviewed had many legitimate reasons for their anger, you too have good cause to be angry. You may feel that you are verbally, emotionally, or physically abused; that your husband totally rejects you sexually. You may be trying to cope with your husband's alcohol or drug abuse, and you may feel trapped in a bad situation and out of control of your life. You may feel that your sexual self is being denied and that you face the choice of living without sex or seeking a new partner in these days when AIDS threatens even heterosexual sex. Or, after years of having your looks or your figure criticized and ridiculed, your self-esteem may be so trampled and crushed it is inconceivable to you that any other man would ever want you.

"But why then," you may ask, "can it be so hard to express my anger constructively? Why do I either clam up and keep quiet about how I feel or end up smashing things, screaming at the kids, or rushing into the kitchen to gorge myself on ice cream?" To answer this question we must look back to our earlier years when we were learning how to be women and how to express our feelings. The clues lie in our culture.

As a result of our upbringing, many women have great difficulty dealing effectively with anger. Until recently most women had few role models who were assertive, aggressive, or effective on the local or national level. In earlier years, the trend-setting media that helped teach girls how to be women placed great emphasis on catching a husband, keeping a tidy home, and, of course, meeting everyone else's needs.

Perhaps when you tried expressing your anger, you were called unladylike or unfeminine, a shrew, a bitch, or a castrator. Who wants to be saddled with such epithets? It is not surprising if you, like so many women, ended up as a nurturer, a caretaker and peacemaker, believing that expressing your anger would rock the boat and the whole family might drown in the process. So you cling to your role as wife or mother or working woman, and you keep silent about your pain and continue to play the charade of "one big happy family" for the benefit of relatives and neighbors. On the surface you appear to have it all together, while you walk around with knots in your stomach, tension headaches, or a hair-trigger temper.

Diana's early upbringing taught her very effectively how to stuff her feelings. "My mother and grandmother were always perfect ladies—well-groomed, soft-spoken, in complete control of their emotions, and wearing a pleasant expression no matter

51

how distasteful the situation. As a child when I would be angry, upset, overly exuberant, or crying, I was always told, 'Little ladies don't act like that.' If my mother and grandmother were angry, and I'm sure they were at times, they dealt with it behind closed doors and I never saw it. The effect this had on me is reflected in what a friend said to me one day, 'You always seem so completely calm. I've never seen you lose your temper, even raise your voice.' She even asked me, 'Are you always like that?'

"What she saw was the quiet Diana stuffing my feelings. My friend didn't see me struggling with anger at home, being either totally passive or, since I could find no comfortable way to express my anger, out of control, throwing things at my husband or trying to scratch him with my fingernails. When his mother asked, 'What happened to you?' he said, 'The cat did it.' "

In this chapter we will help you to identify how angry you are and offer some suggestions for expressing your feelings. However, since so many women do not deal well with anger, we have also devoted all of chapter three to a step-by-step program for handling your anger.

Barbara never learned how to deal positively with her anger. She told us, "After the birth of our daughter I was stunned to discover that Sol considered our children more important than I was. He doted on them, he adored them, and I felt left out, shoved into the background of his life, then and forever. I believed the kids didn't like me. If there was a problem with one of the kids, he'd say, 'I'll go to her. You'll only make her angry,' and I let him. By the time our three children were in college and they phoned home, he would imperiously tell me to 'get off the phone.' "

Through the years Sol continued to criticize and belittle Barbara. "He treated me shoddily. He would say to me, 'Oh, that's not what you mean,' or rudely, 'You didn't mean to say that.' " As Barbara's anger grew, so did her frustration. "I could never talk to him. When we fought he would clam up and go for weeks without talking to me at all. He always had to be right and could never say, 'I'm sorry.' " When Barbara felt that she was going to explode, she took it out on her children. She told us regretfully, "I would go into rages and I would scream and yell at the kids. One thing I really regret was rushing out the door as if I were never coming back. Then I would drive around or sit in the car. I realized later how much that frightened the kids."

One evening after Sol left for a weekend in the country with "the boys," a phone call shattered Barbara's illusions and rudely tore the blinders off. She remembers that night. "I picked up the phone and a woman's voice, like a kick in the stomach, said to me, 'Do you love your husband? He's with my sister.' " Barbara knew. She could name the woman. Provoked to action, she called Sol and demanded he come home at once, and he did. But her confrontation was halfhearted. "I asked him, 'Do you want a divorce?' I counted on his attachment to the children, and to my relief he said 'No.' I hated him for doing this to me. I felt used and abused and was afraid to confront him—to talk to him."

The only way Barbara could express herself to Sol was in a letter. She meekly wrote, "How dare you do this to me? I'm the mother of your children, I cook and clean for you." When Sol read the letter, his nonchalant comment was, "So what?" and he tore it up.

Barbara could not rant and rave at Sol, so she continued to take her anger out on her children. She adjusted the blinders once again and assured herself that the economic advantages of being Sol's wife far outweighed being alone. "I kept my feelings inside me. I never told Sol how I felt and I never told anyone I was celibate," she admitted. "I was ashamed. How could I say that my husband didn't desire me and that he didn't sleep with me anymore?"

Barbara's confidence eroded over the years. She was terrified to live on her own, to give up the economic advantages of her marriage. "I didn't want to give up the lifestyle I loved, working nine months in the business and the summers off playing golf at the club."

Before we discuss anger at greater length, it might be helpful for you to find out how angry you are with your celibate lifestyle. The degree of your anger will indicate whether you can handle it yourself or whether you need to seek professional help. The following is a list of statements we have heard many women make about their anger.

EXERCISE ────────────────────────────

Anger on a Scale of 1 to 18

Number a page in your journal from 1 to 18. Mark True for each statement you agree with or may have thought at some time in your marriage.

1. I often feel angry about not having sex with my husband.
2. I feel deprived of not having a real marriage.
3. I feel jealous of women I know who have a good sex life.
4. I often feel lonely.
5. I don't really have strong feelings about anything anymore.
6. My husband and I seem to argue about any little thing lately.
7. I seem to be eating or drinking more, particularly when I'm angry.
8. I never used to feel angry like this before I was married.
9. Sometimes my anger feels like a bottomless pit.

10. I find myself yelling at the kids frequently—even when they don't really deserve it.
11. Sometimes I wish my husband would just die so I could go on with my life.
12. I've even thought about suicide because I'm so upset over our marriage.
13. My husband and/or I have been physically violent at times.
14. I could honestly say that sometimes I hate my husband.
15. I grew up in an unhappy home.
16. I'm too inhibited to tell my husband how I really feel.
17. I put on a good act so that family and friends won't really know how bad our marriage is.
18. Sometimes I have dreams about hurting my husband.

Go back over your list and look for patterns in your answers. Do you seem to be in a marriage where there is a lot of fighting going on? Do you see that you are taking your anger out in inappropriate ways, like hitting or screaming at your children, or drinking too much? These are danger signals you need to become alert to so that you can make changes in your behavior before it causes serious trouble for you or your family.

If you answered True to 10 or more of the questions, this means that you are very angry and would benefit from outside help. We suggest that you find a counselor or psychologist with whom you feel comfortable talking about your marriage. This person might also help you to feel better about yourself and help you plan for a better future. You will also want to work carefully through chapter three.

If you responded True to less than 10 questions, the two techniques for venting your anger suggested below may be enough for you.

Whether you are the type of celibate wife who stuffs her feelings and suffers in silence, or the type who explodes in verbal or physical rages, it is important for you to vent your anger and rage privately, to get your feelings up and out, before you can attempt to discuss your feelings with your husband rationally and calmly.

We recommend two exercises for getting your feelings out into the open. The first asks you to write a letter you will never mail, in which you will ventilate all your feelings. The second asks you to use a small pillow to physically ventilate your emotions.

EXERCISE
The Unmailed Letter

Write one or several letters to your husband telling him how he has hurt you and how angry you are at him. If you feel violent toward him at times, say so. Write about specific incidents and tell him how it feels to be a celibate wife. This might be the place to threaten to leave him if things don't change. Allow your emotions to flow freely; let yourself groan or cry as you write about your marriage.

You will never mail this letter. The purpose is not to tell your husband how you feel but to express your feelings to yourself. After writing the letter, destroy it. Do not leave it lying around or tucked away in a drawer where he may find it. That could be disastrous at this stage when you are not yet ready to confront him with your feelings about your nonsexual marriage.

EXERCISE
Pillow Pounding

This technique has worked well for many celibate wives, even though you may feel a little silly trying it at first. Look around your house for a small throw pillow, or buy an inexpensive one. In your mind give this pillow your husband's name. When you are expressing your anger at your husband, you will talk to "him," the pillow. One woman we know splashed her husband's aftershave on the pillow to make the effect more realistic.

You need to find a time and place to be alone when you talk to your pillow. Do not do this while your children are in the house. If they hear you crying or yelling, they may become frightened. Of course, you will make sure that your husband is also away for a few hours.

By the time your marriage becomes celibate you probably have years of angry complaints to vent. Find a place in the house where you are comfortable talking to your "husband pillow." Begin to talk to him about how you feel about being a celibate wife. Pour out your hurts and anger. Remind him of specific events in your sex life that were especially unhappy for you. Really let go and yell at him or cry freely. As you feel the anger energy building within you, give yourself permission to let it come out. Feel free to hit or slap the pillow, beat it against something, stomp on it, or throw it at a wall across the room. Curse at the pillow and use any vile or filthy words that come to your mind—they are helpful in expressing anger.

When you feel yourself winding down, you may want to curl up on the couch or your bed and cry for a while or just rest. Chances are you'll be very tired. Use this time to calm down and relax. When you feel ready, put your "husband pillow" away till the next time and congratulate yourself for doing something positive.

How often should you get your "husband pillow" out? As often as you feel the need to let the anger at him flow. Initially you may feel the need to do this several times a week, and then it may slow to once every few weeks. Our awareness of our anger seems to ebb and flow. There will probably be times when you feel relieved that you have finished dealing with your anger, and then you are surprised when another chunk comes rushing up. Sometimes anger feels like a bottomless pit. You may find yourself dealing with anger many times on your walk through the grieving process.

As denial crumbles a piece at a time, so anger is dealt with one chunk at a time. It is a natural, expected, and necessary process. Do not feel guilty or embarrassed by your anger. It is the normal reaction to living in a difficult celibate marriage.

In chapter three we will offer you specific suggestions for dealing directly with your husband about your anger. Before you begin to do that, however, it is best if you have vented much of your anger and rage by one or both of the previously suggested methods. Set aside time soon to write your letters or to talk to your "husband pillow."

MAGICAL THINKING—BARGAINING

The third stage of the grieving process, according to Dr. Kübler-Ross, is that of bargaining. Bargaining is magical thinking for celibate wives. You may believe that you can control something you have no real power over—your husband's behavior.

Bargaining takes many forms. You are not alone if you find that you bargain with God and that you become more faithful in church attendance, prayer, and good works to keep your side of the bargain. You genuinely trust that God will reward your faithfulness with an end to your celibacy and an improvement in your marriage.

Do you sometimes bargain with your husband? For example, you might agree to move to the country, a change you have previously resisted, because you believe then your husband will finally be happy and your marriage and sex life will improve. Perhaps you agree to his buying an expensive new "toy," such as a boat or car you know you can't really afford, because then he'll appreciate your cooperation and love you more.

Do you sometimes bargain with yourself? Do you say, "I'll lose 20 pounds and he'll find me attractive again," or "I'll start working (or quit working) and then we'll get along fine"?

Bargaining can be a "time-out" stage when you are overwhelmed with anger and depression, or a time when you just can't face being alone and totally responsible for your own future. Bargaining is not necessarily negative. It can be useful in that it can temporarily take the pressure off you to make a final decision whether to stay or leave your celibate marriage. It allows you the time to relax, to regroup and hang on in your difficult situation. Bargaining offers hope that your celibacy is not permanent, that you can still change or fix it and your life will be better.

Through the years of their marriage, Barbara's weight fluctuated. She and Sol shared a bitter joke that if Barbara weighed more than 150 pounds, they'd sleep in separate beds. When Barbara lost weight, as she periodically did, Sol was indeed more sexual with her. Yet, over the long haul, dieting was not a cure for their increasingly longer celibate periods or for his infidelity.

Barbara made a deal with herself. She reminded us, "I'm a cockeyed optimist. I had a good man to support me. I decided not to pay attention to what he did or with whom, and I comforted myself with the idea that when the children grew up we would be alone and it would be better."

If you take the time to examine your own behavior, you will undoubtedly find ways in which you, too, bargained and hoped for a return to a good sex life with your partner. When you remember these bargains you might want to write them down in your journal, in order to understand how you have tried to cope with celibacy. Some bargains may amuse you, or you may feel saddened as you realize how much time, energy, and hope you put into this kind of magical thinking.

Joan came to expect no improvement in her sex life, and she bargained with herself in order to stay in the marriage. "I decided, when I was married about eight years, to have an affair in order to stay in the marriage. I was bargaining, not so much for a return to good sex in my marriage, but because I felt Neal was a decent man and I didn't want to break up the children's home. I thought by meeting my sexual needs elsewhere I would satisfy everybody in some way and preserve our marriage. What I discovered was that this didn't solve the celibacy problem: I was as unhappy with this lifestyle as I had been being monogamous and craving sex."

Diana spent many years bargaining with God and feeling guilty and disappointed. "For years I bargained with God. I went to church several times a week, several prayer groups prayed for the marriage, and I worked hard at being more accepting of people, less judgmental, more kind and generous. I really believed God would change Ned into a loving, affectionate, and faithful husband. Then one day I met a new minister who said to me, 'Don't you know why God hasn't changed your husband?' I said, 'No, tell me!' He explained, 'God has given us all free will, including your husband, and God will not force him to be the kind of man or husband that you want.' The burden of not praying right or not praying enough, or being good enough was lifted from my shoulders. I realized then that I couldn't, and God wouldn't, change Ned, and that helped me toward accepting the reality of my celibate marriage."

Accept the fact that bargaining is natural and necessary as

you grieve for the loss of sex in your marriage. Do not berate yourself when you find yourself making yet one more agreement with yourself or with God in the hope of changing things. Moving toward accepting your situation and deciding how to handle it is a two-step-forward, one-step-back process, like any other major change we undertake. Trust that you will move beyond bargaining when you are ready.

Once you accept that bargaining will not bring about change in your husband and you can only change yourself, you can begin to focus on those things that bring you happiness. As you will see in chapter six, you can make new friends, gain self-esteem, and build a whole new life.

FROM THE DEPTHS OF DEPRESSION

When she was asked about depression, Barbara told us that she was never depressed. "I had no time for that. I was involved in the business and there were activities involving my three children, and I had an active social life with friends. I played cards and mah-jongg, and I golfed all summer. I had too busy a life for depression."

Was Barbara denying depression? Yes and no. It was not her nature to give way to despair. She insisted on seeing her glass as always half-full, not half-empty. She believed that she was lucky to be financially secure and she relished that lifestyle. It was important to her that friends and family view her life as a happy one, and she acted as if it were indeed.

But most celibate wives we interviewed spoke of periods of deep depression as they tried to understand and fix their relationships with their husbands. Another common characteristic was that these women almost automatically shouldered the blame for the problems in their sex lives and assumed that it was basically their responsibility to fix them. This may be a clue to the reason for such widespread depression, for these women have undertaken an impossible task. No celibate wife can single-handedly fix her marriage. She needs the active cooperation of her husband, and it must be an important goal for both of them.

As celibate wives move through their denial and face the reality of their situations, when they realize that bargaining is only a temporary time-out and not the answer to their problem, they often begin to experience depression. They feel, "I can't go on living without sex anymore; I feel so sad things worked out this way and I don't know what to do about my future. I feel overwhelmed, confused, and totally unable to cope at times."

If you are experiencing these feelings about your own marriage, remember that this, too, is an expected and necessary part of grieving the loss of sex in your marriage. Rather than thinking of this depression as a pit you may never be able to crawl out of, think of it as a bridge you must cross to get to the happier life you deserve.

Two Faces of Depression

Depression shows itself in both physical and emotional symptoms. It is often the underlying but unrecognized cause when women go to their doctors with a variety of physical symptoms but are never asked about their unhappy marriages or sex life. These women might be said to be suffering masked depression.

There are at least two types of depression, and we need to understand the differences between them so that we can understand what we need to do to help ourselves.

Situational depression results in response to a particular life event, usually a loss of a loved one, loss of a job or a promotion, feeling the closeness to our husbands or children slip away, or the loss of our sex life.

Although situational depression is painful, it usually does not feel all-consuming. You find yourself gradually feeling less depressed over time. Commonsense approaches, such as talking about the loss and keeping active and involved in daily activities, are helpful. At first you may find yourself thinking about your loss off and on all day long, but you gradually find there are days when you haven't thought about it at all. You will know then that you are healing and are doing as much as you need to do to handle your depression.

Joan explains how she handled depression: "There were many days when I would wake up with a heavy heart, but I would force myself out of bed. My primary activity for 10 years, other than my children and their activities, was going to college. It lifted my spirits and became my vocation, my life work, until I obtained a degree. And I found emotional intimacy through strong friendships with women; I was able to talk about my sex problems, and that helped relieve my depression."

The other type, *clinical depression*, seems all-consuming, does not lighten with time, and hinders you from being able to keep up your normal activities. It is more physically based than situational depression and often requires treatment with medication by a doctor.

The following exercise will help you determine if you are presently experiencing depression in your celibate marriage and help you decide if you need professional counseling. In chapter four, "Overcoming Depression," we will provide concrete suggestions that you may implement to feel less depressed and more able to cope with your celibacy.

EXERCISE
The Two Faces of Depression

Number a page in your journal from 1 to 20. Mark True next to each statement that applies to you. Notice that this list contains both physical and emotional symptoms of depression. Think back carefully over the last six months as you consider these statements.

1. There's not much pleasure in my life.
2. I notice I'm having trouble making decisions.
3. I frequently can't get to sleep or I wake up too early.
4. I feel exhausted most of the time.
5. I have a lot of headaches.
6. I'm just not interested in sex anymore.
7. I think about death a lot, my own and others'.
8. I'm having trouble remembering names or other things.
9. My anxiety level seems higher than before.
10. I don't go out much anymore.
11. The slightest little thing irritates me.
12. Sometimes I feel dizzy for no apparent reason.
13. I've thought about suicide at times.
14. Sometimes my heartbeat seems irregular.
15. I frequently feel guilty about what I've done.
16. My back has really bothered me lately.
17. I've lost interest in hobbies and activities.
18. Nothing seems to give me much pleasure these days.
19. I'm too tired to do much lately.
20. It's incredibly hard to get up in the morning.

As you completed this exercise you may have recognized that you are indeed suffering some depression. Do not feel alarmed, upset, or ashamed by this. It is an indication that you are responding like most other celibate wives. With a program of self-help and/or professional help, you will move through your depression toward a time when you feel better and have more energy to make decisions about your marriage.

Now let's look at how depressed you might be. If you

answered True to questions 7 and/or 13, we suggest that you seek professional help immediately. You may be at risk for suicide and no longer able to rely on self-help. Please call your medical doctor, local mental health clinic, or crisis hotline, and be sure to tell them that you think about death and suicide and need to be seen very soon. Do not be distressed at having such thoughts. In chapter four, Diana recalls her period of deep depression and suicidal thoughts. Many celibate wives reach such a low point.

Now back to scoring the exercise. Score one point for each True answer and total your score. If you scored less than 8 points (not including numbers 7 or 13), you are probably not experiencing much depression at this time.

If you marked True to mostly those items regarding physical symptoms, you might find it helpful to take this list to your doctor and see if he or she believes your physical complaints are related to depression and what treatment might be advisable.

If you answered more than eight questions true, you are indeed suffering from depression in your celibate marriage. You will want to read and work through chapter four carefully.

For any depressed celibate wife our first recommendation, again, is that you break the silence and begin to talk about your (probably secret) celibacy. Find a friend or counselor whom you feel you can trust with the intimate details of your life. As you begin to talk about your marriage, you may initially feel more depressed. This is because you have finally begun to deal openly and honestly with your celibate marriage. Don't let this discourage you. Continue talking and getting your feelings up and out, for this is the way we all heal and move through our mourning process.

You might also find it helpful to write your feelings in your journal. You might do this whenever you start feeling depressed and do not have someone available to talk to. Let your feelings of sadness flow onto the page. Allow yourself to experience your emotions, and take as much time as you need. Return to this journaling when you remember other ways you've been hurt in your marriage or are feeling particularly depressed.

REACHING ACCEPTANCE

There will probably come a time when you have taken off your blinders of denial, stopped bargaining to change your husband, expressed much of your anger and depression, and you can look more calmly and clearly at your celibate marriage. You can trace your path to celibacy, acknowledging the mistakes both you and your husband made along the way. These are indications that you have completed much of your grief work and are reaching the stage of acceptance.

Let's be clear about what acceptance really is. It is not saying to yourself, "I guess that's just the way my marriage is. I can't do anything about it; all I can do is take it one day at a time." This fatalistic approach will only lead you to more anger and further depression. Acceptance is a state of mind, a way of thinking about and seeing things as they really are, not the way you necessarily want them to be.

True acceptance is saying to yourself, "I accept my husband as he is and know that I don't have the power to change him. I also accept that I cannot single-handedly fix our marriage." Acceptance is being free to stay, free to go. Acceptance is deciding to focus on your own needs and behavior and build a good life for yourself *in or out* of this marriage. With acceptance comes a state of detachment. Formerly painful situations no longer elicit the powerful negative emotions that caused you pain.

Barbara did not realize she had reached the stage of acceptance until her husband asked for a divorce. Sol became ill and was hospitalized. From his sickbed he announced he wanted a divorce. "I was shocked," Barbara remembered. "One of my daughters standing by the bed said, 'That would be the best thing for Mom.' I was furious with her. My first reaction was, 'I'm going to fight for him.' But after Sol came home, and I had time to think about my life, I realized that since he wanted out, my financial benefits would be good. The steam went out of me—what was the point of going on like this? I said, 'Okay, get out now,' and he did. Don't think I wasn't terrified. But it didn't last long."

In the 12 years since her divorce, Barbara has enjoyed a wonderful, sexually satisfying romance. She has been successful at work and established more honest and deeper relationships with her children. Unburdened from the game of "Isn't my life wonderful?" Barbara has used her creativity and energy to build a meaningful, enjoyable life for herself.

Because reaching the stage of acceptance helps you to think more clearly, you may begin to plan for your future. Now is the time to think back over your life to look for patterns of what brings you a sense of happiness and fulfillment. Is it learning new skills, working at an interesting job, or perhaps being involved with children? Do you prefer living in a calm and peaceful environment, or the stimulation of a big city? Would you like more time to pursue your favorite hobby? Once you identify the things that bring you happiness, you can plan ways of bringing them into your life on a regular basis.

When you have completed much of your grieving, feel more in control of your life and as a result feel better about yourself, and are doing things that make you happy, then you should sit down and decide how you want to solve the problem of your celibate marriage.

You may find that your husband is also interested in restoring good sex to your marriage. You will find the stories of the couples in chapter five, who were able to put the sizzle back into sex, encouraging.

On the other hand, you may decide to file for divorce and strike out on your own, as did the women in chapter six. Or you may decide that there are elements more important than the loss of sex in your marriage, and you may have good reasons to stay. If so, the stories of the women in chapter seven will particularly interest you. Whatever your decision, because you have worked through the stages of the grieving process, you will be better able to make a plan for your life and follow through with it.

Remember that you have many sisters in celibate marriages who share your feelings and dreams. We have encouraged and applauded many celibate wives as they worked through grieving their lost sexuality and crafted happy futures for themselves.

CHAPTER 3

DEALING WITH ANGER

* MARIE
I wrote him a letter, which I never mailed. It said, "Dom, I never knew what hate was until these last few years. I hate you. You've hurt me for the last time, you no-good bastard."

* CAMILLA
I felt slimed. My doctor said, "You have a venereal disease—do you know where you got it?" Yes, I knew. My husband had infected me. God knows who he'd been screwing. I was enraged. I ended our sex life, then I felt deprived and even angrier.

* DIANA
After we were celibate, Ned flaunted his women in my face. He would bring home letters and cards from his girlfriends and receive phone calls at home from them. Beneath the deep sadness I felt, my rage smoldered and took its toll on my body through a series of illnesses.

Anger in marriage is nothing to be minimized. Turn on the nightly news in many medium-sized towns or large cities and you will hear of married men and women committing unspeakable acts of violence on each other. According to FBI statistics, every 15 seconds a woman is physically abused by her husband and every 6 hours a man beats his wife to death.

Marie, an attractive 31-year-old housewife and mother of two, told us that she felt she had not yet recovered from the physical and emotional trauma of her 11-year marriage to Dom. "I guess I had hints, even before we were married, that Dom was potentially violent. He had a knee-jerk temper. I've seen him get out of a car to curse another driver, or reduce a salesperson to tears. He once grabbed me and shook me in front of the kids, who started screaming before he let me go.

"About six years into the marriage," Marie revealed, "Dom started staying out very late and would answer no questions about his behavior. I hated him to kiss me, reeking as he was with stale liquor and a perfume that wasn't mine. When I tried to talk to him about it he just turned on the TV and ignored me. I began to go to bed earlier and to sleep at the far edge of the bed. I'd complain of a backache or of being too exhausted, anything to avoid sex with him."

One Saturday night after they got home from a party, Dom accused Marie of flirting with her best friend's husband and became enraged when she spurned his sexual advances. He smacked her face, wrenched her breast, and forced himself on her. When he finished he walked out, leaving Marie curled on her side of the bed in a fetal position, hurting all over. Marie didn't know where Dom was for two days. Her face clouded with pain as she recalled, "Six weeks later I was sickened to find out that I was pregnant. I didn't want a baby conceived in such pain and anger, yet I felt guilty rejecting this innocent baby."

Marie presented a smile to the world and went through the motions of living although she felt used and betrayed. Shortly thereafter she was diagnosed with an ulcer. Marie told no one about her situation. In her Catholic, Italian family, divorce was inconceivable. She felt trapped.

During one particularly devastating night of violence. "Dom came home late. I had been watching TV, and when he stumbled through the door knocking over the coat stand, I suddenly felt such rage I rushed after him up the steps screaming at his back, 'You bastard, look at me! Who the hell do you think you are dragging your stinking self in here after being with God knows who? I'm sick of you.' He turned and shoved me. I fell down the stairs and landed so hard on the tile floor that I was unconscious. Later that night I lost the baby. Dom never came to the hospital. I was just as glad. I was scared of him and I hated him. When I got home I said to him, 'If you ever touch me again I'll tell my father and brothers what you did and they'll take care of you.'"

Marie plunged into immobilizing depression. "What a mess I was at 30, frighteningly angry, celibate, depressed, and with a painful ulcer."

Marie and Dom remained celibate and avoided each other except for required family activities for more than a year. He left for work earlier and hardly ever came home for dinner. Marie kept herself busy with her daughters' activities and church over the weekends when Dom was home. She was afraid to trigger his violent temper. They never again spoke of the night she "fell" down the stairs.

One night Dom came home late and got into their bed reeking of perfume and liquor. Marie recounted, "I hated him more and more for sleeping with other women. I hated him for the way he'd changed. As I listened to his snoring, I began to feel rage welling up inside of me; I wanted to smash him and hurt him as he hurt me all those years. I began to fantasize about how I could kill him while he slept. I could imagine myself getting up and getting the gun he kept on the closet shelf. I knew if I didn't get out of there I might do it. I grabbed my bathrobe and slippers and rushed downstairs and out the front door. It was freezing cold, and I walked up and down the street crying. I must have looked as deranged as I felt. By the time I calmed down my feet felt like ice cubes, as frozen as my heart, and I knew that I had to get out of that marriage no matter what happened."

It is easy to understand why dealing with her anger was so difficult for Marie. She didn't know how to handle her rage and felt overwhelmed and frightened by its intensity. She knew she had come close to murdering Dom yet was afraid to talk to him about a separation.

THE CHANGING FACE OF ANGER

In the 1940s and 1950s women who expressed anger were often labeled unstable, immature, or hysterical and were treated with numbing tranquilizers.

Then, in the late 1960s and early 1970s, women (as well as men) were told to "let it all hang out." A healthy emotional climate was described by Dr. Theodore Rubin in his *Angry Book* as "one in which all the emotions—especially anger—are given ample play and freedom." But several studies of family violence found verbal aggression and physical aggression to be closely related. This means that yelling may intensify anger; it may be followed by a slap; the other partner may grab a weapon—and we have another gruesome incident of family violence. Marie was terrified by how close she had come to being a statistic.

Thankfully, anger has been researched extensively and a more carefully reasoned approach, called reflection, is now recommended. This means waiting until you and the person who has made you angry calm down and then trying to reason with him.

Carol Tavris, in her excellent book *Anger: The Misunderstood Emotion*, explains the importance of taking a cooling-off period before dealing with anger:

> The psychological rationale for ventilating anger does not stand up under experimental scrutiny. The weight of the evidence indicates precisely the opposite: expressing anger makes you angrier, solidifies an angry attitude, and establishes a hostile habit. If you keep quiet about momentary irritation and distract yourself with pleasant activity until your fury simmers down, chances are you will feel better, and feel better faster, than if you let yourself go in a shouting match.

Reflection, waiting for tempers to cool down before discussing the issues, has traditionally been a female approach to resolving conflict. There does seem to be evidence that women's less explosive way of dealing with anger is effective. This does not mean that women are afraid to stand up for their rights or that they enjoy being treated like doormats.

Marie began to see a counselor at a women's center, and she joined our group of celibate wives. Initially she sat in stony silence, her arms wrapped around her body clutching her elbows, listening intently as other women shared their feelings.

When Marie finally opened up, her anger poured out like a flood. "I feel so cheated. It's not fair. I don't deserve to be living without love, without sex, and to be so scared and miserable. What's so awful is that I really enjoyed sex. When I had my first orgasm I couldn't believe anything could feel so good. But after Dom hit me and raped me, I cringed at the thought of his ever touching me again."

We began to teach Marie our plan for dealing with anger. The DIAL program is a four-step plan that provides a constructive method of working with anger. It was devised by Diana at a time when she was having great difficulty dealing with her angry feelings about her celibacy. Ned would either become enraged or walk away when she tried to tell him how she felt. The DIAL plan provided Diana with a way of coping with her intense emotions and enabled her to confront situations while feeling fully in control of her behavior.

Diana explains, "I had to find a way to approach him so that he would listen to me, because I had a right to express my feelings about the celibacy in our marriage. I learned to carefully pick my time and place for our discussions, and I had learned in counseling classes how to stick to 'I' statements that would not make him feel blamed or attacked. I found that it was important to acknowledge his feelings and to talk about my hurt or pain in the relationship rather than my anger. I discovered we were more likely to reach a compromise with this approach, and I found that giving him a little hug and a smile when we finished contributed to our both feeling positive about our talk. The DIAL model didn't save my marriage, but it made it much easier to talk with Ned about our problems and to negotiate the details of our separation."

As you worked through chapter two, we hope you took the time to ventilate many of your angry feelings by writing (but not mailing) letters to your husband and/or talking to your "husband pillow." Ventilating your anger in these safe ways is absolutely essential before you begin to work with the DIAL program. Otherwise you may try to talk with your husband calmly and rationally, only to find yourself still out of control, yelling and screaming about things that happened months or even years before.

When we felt that Marie was ready, that she had ventilated her anger through writing anguished and acrimonious letters to Dom (which she burned), we rehearsed each step in the DIAL plan with her: how and when she would approach Dom and the actual phrases she would use to tell him she wanted a separation. About six months after we met her, Marie discussed separation with Dom and he agreed without a fuss, to her relief and astonishment. Because they are Catholic, divorce is out of the question, but Marie is happy with her new job working in the office of her uncle's car dealership, and she and her daughters are starting to feel settled and relaxed as a threesome.

As Marie mastered the DIAL plan, she practiced using it with anyone with whom she had a disagreement—her children, a co-worker, even the mechanic who fixed her car. The more she practiced, the easier it became, until it was almost second nature for her to respond to anger in this way. Here is how the DIAL plan works.

Dial Away Anger

STEP 1

"D" Means Delay

When your husband (or anyone else for that matter) does something that makes you angry, don't let go with your own blast of anger. *Delay your response* until you have calmed down. Force yourself to think about something else or to do something that you enjoy. Sing your favorite song, take a walk, remember the best time you ever had. By taking your mind off the unpleasant incident, you will gradually calm down. If you allow yourself to keep thinking about what happened, replaying it again and again in your mind, you will only keep feeling angry. When you delay your response and calm down, you will have a sense of control over your situation, a sense that is missing when the anger starts flying. Observe the other person and see if he has calmed down. Only when there is emotional calm can you consider taking step two. Make sure you have calmed down to the point where your gestures, facial expressions, and tone of voice match your calm words and will not provoke an angry reply. You may decide to wait hours or even days before you discuss what happened. Just as you will carefully choose the words you will use, you should also carefully choose the time and place where this discussion will take place.

STEP 2

"I" Means Making "I" Statements

When you think you are both calm enough to talk rationally about what happened, carefully phrase what you say in the form of "I," "We," or "Our" statements. Avoid "You" statements, which point the finger of blame on the other person.

Since sex is so highly emotional a subject, we will look at an exchange between Marie and Dom on a less volatile subject first.

Marie: "I was very embarrassed when I found that I didn't have enough money to pay for all the groceries yesterday. I try hard to budget the money you give me, but the girls needed money for their dance recital costumes and that left me short of cash. I felt humiliated as I had to stand there at the checkout counter in front of all those people, sorting out those things that weren't absolutely necessary. I understand that you are working very hard and the trucking business has been difficult this year, but the expenses for the girls seem to keep going up as they get older, so we need to take another look at my monthly household budget. Will you please sit down with me Saturday morning and help me write a more reasonable budget to cover these additional expenses for the girls?"

Read this scene again. Notice how Marie sticks to "I" statements. She avoids blaming Dom. She asks for his ideas how to solve the problem.

Contrast this with what Marie might have said before she learned the four-step DIAL plan. She might have confronted Dom in this way:

"I could have just died when I didn't have enough cash at the grocery store. You never give me enough money. You're stingy, just like your father. I don't care if business is rough this year. I won't be embarrassed like that again."

This would immediately have put Dom on the defensive, and an angry shouting match might have resulted. Don't fall into the trap of making statements like, "I think you . . ." or "I know you . . ." These start with the word "I" but usually end up being "you" statements that point the blame at the other person.

STEP 3

"A" Means Pay Attention to Your Hurts, Not Your Anger

In the first scenario, notice that Marie paid attention to, focused on, and identified her hurts rather than her anger. She said:

a. *I* was embarrassed.
b. *I* felt humiliated.
c. *I* try hard, but I'm short of cash.

Dealing with anger is like peeling an onion: peel away enough layers and you reveal the hurt that underlies most anger. Focus on the hurt when you discuss your unhappiness with your husband. If you can share your hurts, you may make real progress toward understanding each other's pain and expressing your concern for each other. This could help you understand the celibacy in your marriage, no matter what your ultimate decision is about your future.

STEP 4

"L" Means End with a Loving Gesture

End your discussion with a loving gesture, whether it's a hug or kiss or just a smile and handshake. This is a thank-you for working things out and an encouragement to calmly discuss things in the future. Marie was able to smile at Dom when they finished talking about the budget, but she didn't feel like hugging or kissing him. She put a plate of his favorite cookies on the table and they chatted comfortably about the girls as they shared the cookies. This was a nice way of expressing her appreciation to Dom for sitting down and working things out.

We are not assuming or implying that it will be easy to get your husband to sit down and discuss your celibate marriage. We understand from personal experience that some husbands are so unable to talk about their feelings that they will change the subject, walk out of the room, or respond in anger rather than face their suppressed hurts and fears. Don't nag your husband about opening up to you, but don't give up too easily. Changes in behavior take time. As you model this way of dealing with anger to your family, they may gradually begin to use it also. Don't use this DIAL model to discuss emotionally loaded subjects like sex and divorce with your husband until you have mastered it with different people and in different situations.

There have probably been times when you dealt inappropriately with your husband about something he did that made you angry. Maybe you clammed up and said nothing about your anger, so nothing was resolved. Or maybe you blasted your husband with your anger so that he lashed out at you or just walked off and ignored you. Again, nothing constructive was accomplished. With the following exercise you will begin to understand and practice a more effective way of expressing your anger.

EXERCISE
Mental DIALing

Think of an argument you have recently had with your husband and replay it in your mind. Mentally rewrite the script as we guide you through the four-step DIAL process.

STEP 1
Delay Your Response

When would have been a good time to talk about it after you had calmed down? Where would you have been most comfortable discussing this? We don't recommend your bedroom with its possible connotations of past pleasures or present pains. Meeting on the back patio, taking a walk together, or sitting at the kitchen table when no one else is home are more neutral settings.

STEP 2
Make "I" Statements

How could you have used "I," "We," and "Our" statements rather than "You" statements that seem to blame or accuse your partner? Write down a few "I" statements that might have been helpful.

STEP 3
Pay Attention to Hurts, Not Anger

Think back past your anger to recall what you were really feeling. Were you feeling hurt, scared, embarrassed, inadequate, rejected, lonely? It's important that you express not the anger, but what you were really feeling. Take one or two of these feelings and write "I" statements about them. An example might be, "I feel crushed when you yell at me," or "I feel lonely when you don't come home for dinner." Using "I" statements, you tell the other person how you are feeling. Do not begin with "You hurt me . . ." Do begin with, "I feel hurt . . ." It is possible for you to learn to express your anger calmly and effectively.

Finish with a Loving Gesture

Think about how you might say thank-you to your partner for taking the time to sit, listen, and talk with you. Would you feel comfortable giving him a hug or a pat on the back? Maybe you could bring out the cookies, like Marie did.

Apply the DIAL plan to several different situations. Your goal is to understand the plan and become comfortable using it. You can learn to be assertive rather than passive or aggressive. We have seen passive celibate wives who could express almost no anger begin to experience their sense of personal power as they stated their true feelings in situations with their husbands. We have also seen overly aggressive women go from raging anger and physical outbursts to calmly expressing their hurts and fears, as they mastered our DIAL plan.

Take Your Anger Out of Cold Storage

We are not suggesting that you swallow your feelings of anger. You may have spent years trying to ignore or repress your sexuality, and this can generate great anger. You may, as many women described to us, "feel dead inside," and you may be missing the joys and highs of life as well as the lows.

Dr. Rubin explains this phenomenon:

In removing ourselves from our feelings—that is, submerging and deadening our feelings—we are extraordinarily destructive to ourselves. This is a form of self-imposed anesthesia like ether or gas that kills our spontaneity, sensitivity, and potential creativity. It is the great destroyer of self, and human identity and human relatedness. How can we relate if we don't feel? We cannot feel with a frozen finger and we cannot feel with frozen emotions. As with a frozen limb, an emotional gangrene sets in which, in feeling tone, removes us from humanity and other people.

As we interviewed Camilla we realized that she had frozen her anger at her husband, Ron, under a facade of smiling composure. Camilla's sex life ended abruptly after 16 years of marriage. She said she can still hear her gynecologist gravely saying to her, "I'll have to treat you for a venereal disease."

"I broke into a cold sweat," Camilla told us. "I could feel this lump squeezing my throat. I wanted to scream or cry. My thinking was confused and I couldn't accept the awful truth that Ron must have been screwing around and brought home a venereal disease. I felt slimed."

Sex for Camilla meant intimacy and the relaxation that orgasms afforded her. She enjoyed sex and had been confident about her skills in bed. The very idea of celibacy filled her with anger.

She was further enraged when she confronted Ron, who stared indifferently at her and said, "Well, so?" She was astounded by Ron's anger when she refused to have sex with him. "How could he expect me to put myself at risk with him again, especially as he offered no explanation nor made any move to get treatment himself? When I thought about his attitude I felt a volcanic explosion waiting to happen in my body." She might have looked for sex outside her marriage, but with AIDS making headlines, Camilla felt, "Sex isn't worth dying for."

Camilla explained how she tried to cope. "I rationalized that priests, nuns, and others had evidently found ways to accommodate to celibacy. But inwardly I was seething with rage because living without sex was more difficult than I had imagined. Masturbation relieved some of the sexual tension, but there was nothing to replace the touching and holding—that's what was important to me.

"The week before my period was the worst. I had very erotic dreams. I got really horny, and almost any man started to look attractive to me. I woke up in the middle of the night having orgasms. I didn't know women had wet dreams. Is that weird? But that's when I became even more enraged at my husband. I'd say to myself,'I hate you, you bastard!' To lie in the same bed next to a man who is capable of having an erection and making love but to have to live celibately because of his promiscuity was more than I could tolerate."

Camilla's anger, held underground for so long, was about to explode. She had almost no time at home alone and found herself driving aimlessly around town trying to calm down rather than yell at her kids. Or she would rush out of the house when she was furious with Ron and go alone to sit on the beach at night.

Camilla opened her heart to us. "I'm often so angry it's hard for me to be nice to people, and I find myself being nasty to drivers in traffic. Even the dog knows when to stay out of my way."

We expressed concern that she might be putting herself in physical danger by going to a beach alone at night or driving while angry, and we suggested that she find a therapist to help her safely express her feelings.

It took a few sessions with a therapist before Camilla trusted her enough to let down her mask of composure and started being honest about how angry and hurt she felt. She was able to yell and scream out her submerged rage, and her therapist encouraged her to beat on one of the couch pillows in the office pretending that it was Ron. Camilla screamed, "You bastard, how could you treat me like that? I hate your guts. I want to hurt you as much as you hurt me!" She hit the pillow again and again crying, "I hate you! I hate you," until she collapsed sweating and exhausted. Camilla reflected, "Gradually I started to feel better about myself. I felt less like a victim and started to feel in control of my life. Somehow I felt lighter too and had more energy; I didn't realize how much of my energy went into holding that rage inside myself."

Camilla decided to make a change, but she needed time to finish a degree in nursing she had halfway completed. Her studies became her passion as she doubled up on her schedule in order to graduate earlier. Camilla has consulted a lawyer and plans divorce as soon as she is employed full time. "Never again," she swears, "will I allow myself to be economically dependent on a man and at his mercy for everything."

Today Camilla sees her therapist occasionally, focusing mostly on her plans for divorce, how to help her children through that difficult time, and understanding what had attracted her to Ron in the first place so that she can avoid marrying a philanderer like him again. Like most women we interviewed, Camilla felt she should have seen signs of what was to come in her marriage. Before they married, Ron treated her with little respect and flirted with other women. Two days before their wedding, he confessed that he'd slept with another woman. "A parting shot," he'd called it. Camilla had smugly told her girlfriends, "I'll keep him so busy after we're married he won't have time to look at other women."

Both Marie and Camilla felt overwhelmed by their anger

and were open to seeking professional help. You may find after using the self-help models in chapters two and three that you need further help. You may feel that seeking such help is a sign of weakness—that you should be able to learn to handle anger on your own. On the contrary, knowing your limitations and seeking professional help is a sign of strength in a woman who cares about herself and her future.

Anger is not the only stumbling block you need to overcome as you move through your grieving process. You can get stuck in depression and find yourself so immobilized that you are unable to lift yourself out of it. Chapter four will help you recognize and understand depression. When you become more aware of depression's warning signs, you can find new ways of moving through your dark night of the soul.

CHAPTER 4

OVERCOMING
DEPRESSION

✳ GAIL

I didn't realize I was depressed even though I was so distracted I was afraid to drive. I was missing appointments and I just could not retain anything. I was afraid that I might have a brain tumor or Alzheimer's.

✳ DIANA

I was so depressed that dying was starting to look more appealing than living. I had even created a plan as to how I might commit suicide. That's when I became really frightened and knew that I needed help quickly.

Depression is an expected stage in grieving the loss of sex in a marriage, but it is a stage where many women get bogged down. However you try to cope, you often feel as if you are stuck in quicksand, or that you are moving without direction through a deepening fog. You need help to process your feelings, to call them up and express them, before you can decide what is best for your life. No matter how hopeless or helpless you may feel, there is no reason to fear that depression is untreatable. In the following pages we will help you identify how severe your depression is and where you can turn for help.

As you have thought more about your celibate marriage, no longer able to deny that the celibacy may be permanent, and as you have begun to face the decision to stay in the marriage or leave, you may feel even more deeply depressed. You may have (thankfully) passed beyond the stage of raging anger, and you may no longer make bargains in hopes your husband will change, but the nagging depression engendered by facing the truth of your celibate marriage just won't let go of you. You may despair of ever again having the energy and clear head necessary to make effective decisions in your life.

You are not alone. Many celibate wives struggle for years to overcome their depression. Friends and family may question why you continue to stay in an obviously unhappy marriage, saying things like, "Just get out of there, you'll be better off on your own." They don't understand how debilitating depression can be.

It would be far too simple to say that celibacy causes depression or that depression causes celibacy; the issue is much more complex. Usually by the time you identify your depression, you have experienced a series of shattering blows to your self-esteem, self-confidence, and sense of control over your life. Most of your hopes and dreams for marriage have been destroyed, and you have probably experienced long periods without sex. You may despair of ever having a better life. The burden of keeping up appearances for family and friends may have further exhausted you. Is it surprising that some days, just getting out of bed and facing the day is a victory?

Gail's struggle to function is typical of many women who are depressed. "At first I functioned like a robot. I went to my volunteer part-time job as a docent at the art museum, and I chauffeured the kids. I cooked, I ate, I existed, without recognizing that my problem was severe depression."

Gail described her marriage as one in which "I turned over control of my life to Marc, a CPA for a large organization. I accepted that he was wise and intelligent, because I had a very poor self-image and felt very dependent. Marc thrived on my dependency. He did the grocery shopping, controlled the money, and set up rules by which we ate, slept, and lived our lives. He treated me as if I were completely incompetent, as if my intuitive approach didn't make sense, as if I just didn't understand how the world worked."

Gail experienced sex as "rigid, inhibited, silent, and unsatisfactory." When, after 17 years of marriage, she began to exert some control over her life, it was by going to bed late, sleeping at the far edge of the bed, and refusing Marc's advances. Finally she moved into a room of her own. Celibacy was Gail's first attempt to stand up to Marc and take charge of some part of her life—her physical body. "When I stopped sleeping with him, for a little while I had a sense of control over my life and felt less depressed. Then, as if losing control in one area scared him, he tightened up on the rest, demanding an accounting not only of every cent spent, but where I went, what I did and with whom, and, if he could have managed it, my thoughts. Any small infraction of one of his endless rules, such as never touching the many piles of his papers and books, or what time we had our meals, could result in raging anger at me and the kids.

"I was almost immobilized for about three years," Gail told us. "I lost all interest in activities like swimming, which I had loved. I functioned with the kids at a bare minimum, and I was afraid to even drive. I'd forget appointments. I couldn't retain anything, and I was terrified that I might have a brain tumor or early Alzheimer's. I finally saw a therapist, and later sharing my feelings in a women's group helped me understand the cause of my depression. Much of the depression lifted when I started to plan a future without Marc."

If Gail's descriptions of "functioning as a robot" or "just existing" ring true for you, don't despair. We will help you to assess how serious your depression is and suggest appropriate sources of help.

LEAPING THE FIRST HURDLE

Mistakenly, many women insist, "When I solve the problems in my marriage I'll feel less depressed." This was Gail's approach to her situation, and she endured years of unnecessary struggle while she lacked the energy and clarity of mind to leave her destructive marriage. What women should say instead is, "I'll deal with my depression first, and then I'll be able to decide how to handle the problems in my marriage."

In his excellent book, *From Glad to Sad*, Nathan S. Kline explains the immobilization that often shackles celibate wives.

Severely stricken depressives can become so down and out mentally and emotionally that they cannot manage the most mundane problems of everyday life. How, then, can they summon the emotional energy to confront painful and critical matters? And how can they reach sensible, practical decisions on important questions that may influence the entire future course of their lives?

Diana is a perfect example of the debilitating effects of depression. She suffered for several years, struggling to stay in her celibate marriage until her children were grown, as her lawyer had advised. After discovering Ned's infidelities she had declared sex to be out of bounds. She marks this point as the beginning of her deep depression. "I just didn't have any strength. I was exhausted whether I had had a good night's sleep or not. I got up in the morning—mornings were the pits—and the day's activities loomed over me and seemed truly overwhelming. Every little thing became a big effort. My children's smiles and little antics no longer brought joy to my life. I lost interest in community activities and hobbies that had brought me real pleasure. I felt like a piece of driftwood that had been battered by the waves, washed ashore, stranded, and left to rot, and through it all I berated myself for not being able to make a decision and act on it."

It was not until Diana realized that healing her depression first was essential to clearer decision-making that she was able to take steps toward leaving her marriage. She sought treatment, part of which included taking medication for depression. The medication worked wonders; her depression disappeared, and for the first time in years Diana could sleep well, think clearly, and view the future with hope.

Our advice to you is to decide not to decide for now. Put off any decision about whether you should stay or leave your marriage. Admit that because of your depression you are in no condition to make decisions about the rest of your life. You do not have the energy necessary to make clear plans. Any thought of the work involved in making major changes in your life (and perhaps in the lives of your children) may seem daunting, so just let it go for now and concentrate on getting help for your depression so that you can feel better.

Make a promise to make yourself number one for now. Put your needs and feelings first for a while. Take a small step by letting go of any unnecessary responsibilities. Can you work fewer hours? Can you give up your role as Girl Scout leader for a few months? Can you turn the responsibility for cooking dinner over to your husband or teenager one or more nights a week? You will need to explain to the family that your depression is an illness, and that you will need their help and cooperation while you work at getting better.

FAMILY AND FRIENDS: HELP OR HINDRANCE?

You may find, as Diana did, that your husband and family are not sympathetic about your depression. Your husband may take your depression as a personal affront, as if you have chosen to feel and act this way. He may become angry or verbally abusive, especially if your exhaustion and lack of interest in activities interferes with his social life.

Because you are no longer able to provide the same level of concern and service as you did before you became depressed—meeting everyone's needs and juggling your many roles of wife, mother, housekeeper, chauffeur, and so on—your children, especially teenagers, may also react with anger. They may become excessively demanding and noncooperative. They may claim that you are not acting as a good mother should.

Your lack of energy and enthusiasm may be interpreted as

rejection or lack of interest by family or friends. They often feel helpless in the face of your depression, and they say and do all the wrong things as far as you are concerned. They may tell you to "shape up" or "just put a smile on your face" or make other equally unhelpful suggestions. You may become even more depressed as you realize how little family or friends understand how you feel. Family and friends cannot be objective about your depression. They are too closely related to your life.

Your depression may also frighten your family. Children can feel especially vulnerable when Mommy is having a hard time. If your children are little, give them lots of hugs and as much attention as possible. Try to find other family members or friends to give them extra time and attention. Your husband, Grandma, or a neighbor might be able to take the children out on Saturday afternoons, for example.

If your children are older than seven or eight, you might be surprised how aware they are about what is going on in the family. Plan time to sit down with them and explain that you are depressed, and let them know a little bit of what that feels like. Explain that you are taking steps to get better and assure them that this state won't go on forever. Answer their questions as completely as you feel comfortable doing. Remember that children have very active imaginations and might be worrying that things are worse than they really are.

As difficult as conditions are in your marriage, your family may resist your getting healthy because change is sometimes frightening. They know you as you are now, but they don't know what you'll be like when you are emotionally healthy. Your husband particularly, and other family members as well, may try to sabotage your efforts to help yourself and to make changes in the family. Hold fast to your decision to take care of yourself and do whatever is necessary to overcome your depression.

WHERE DO YOU GO FROM HERE?

The first step in getting help is for you to decide how depressed you are. To help you make this evaluation we have developed a Depression Self-Test listing four categories of depression. Using this test you will gain greater awareness of just how depressed you are. The Depression Treatment Scale that follows it will guide you to the best sources of help.

EXERCISE ───────────────────────

Depression Self-Test

In your journal write the heading of each of the four categories and number 1 to 4 below each one. As you read the statements under each category, circle in your journal the numbers of the statements that apply to you. Trust yourself and go with your first impulse—don't spend a lot of time debating whether an item is true for you.

LIGHT DEPRESSION
1. My depression lasts several days to several weeks.
2. I have few eating or sleep disturbances.
3. I am able to keep up with normal daily activities.
4. My depression gradually feels better over time.

DEEPER DEPRESSION
1. My depression lasts up to several months.
2. I have significant trouble eating and/or sleeping.
3. I may need to let go of some activities temporarily.
4. I feel better after talking about my marriage with friends or a therapist.

SERIOUS DEPRESSION
1. My depression has lasted months to years.
2. Eating or sleeping problems make it difficult for me to keep up with my activities.

3. I feel overwhelmed and am unable to cope with family or work responsibilities.
4. My depression has not responded to "talking" therapies.

SUICIDAL DEPRESSION

1. My depression may be of short or long duration.
2. I have frequent thoughts of death, my own or that of others.
3. I have given up hope for a better life.
4. I have a plan that may seem reasonable to end my life.

Look in your journal at the four levels of depression and identify in which categories you have the most numbers circled. Refer to the scale below. Your responses will probably be concentrated in one or two levels. Many celibate wives we interviewed had experienced one, several, or all of these degrees of depression.

The Depression Treatment Rating Scale

Think of help for depression as drawn out along a continuum. At the left is help for people with light depression. The degree of help increases as we move to the right, with help for very serious depression at the far right.

The chart on the following page relates the severity of your depression to the kind of help you need to get now that you have identified the point on the continuum where your depression falls. Below the line are the differing types of treatment for depression, corresponding with the type of depression for which they most likely would be used. Two or three types of treatment may be used concurrently in some cases. For instance, if you are in individual therapy your counselor may also refer you to a doctor for medication and invite you to join a support group.

Light Depression	Deeper Depression	Serious Depression	Suicidal Depression
Group therapy	Individual therapy	Medication	Hospitalization

1. LIGHTER DEPRESSION

   If you find that your circles appeared mostly under *Lighter Depression*, you may be adequately helped by a women's support group. Call your mental health clinic, women's center, local YWCA, or church and ask them about women's support groups. Your local newspaper may carry a list of support groups available in your community. We found that a self-help group comprised of celibate wives was especially helpful since we could easily relate to one another's experiences and feelings. In chapter eight you will learn more about groups for celibate wives and how you may form one.

2. DEEPER DEPRESSION

   If you checked several or all of the symptoms listed under *Deeper Depression*, you may benefit most from individual counseling. (For suggestions on finding a counselor, see the Appendix.) It is important for you to feel good about your relationship with your therapist, to trust her or him enough to talk about your innermost feelings, and to feel that you are making progress and building a better future for yourself whether you remain in your celibate marriage or leave.

3. SERIOUS DEPRESSION

   If you checked several symptoms under *Serious Depression*, you need to seek help right away. (See the Appendix for suggestions as to where and how to seek help.) You may need individual therapy as well as medication. Diana and several other celibate wives we talked with credited medication with making remarkable changes in their outlooks on life within several weeks' time.

4. SUICIDAL DEPRESSION

If you have checked any of the symptoms under *Suicidal Depression*, you must reach out for help immediately. (See the Appendix.) The most effective way to help yourself may be to admit that you cannot do it alone. Never be afraid to get help for depression. There are times in our lives when we need someone to point out to us that we still have power, and being depressed is one of those times.

After taking the Depression Self-Test, Gail recognized how deeply depressed she was. She sought individual therapy, became part of a church-sponsored women's support group, and later joined our celibate wives self-help group. With each experience she felt cared for, supported, encouraged, and less depressed. As her confidence grew, Gail began to take charge of her life. She insisted that she was going to earn her nursing degree even if it took several years, and she decided to take a part-time job. She recalled, "These were strong moves for me, and I bent over backward to make concessions to Marc's anger and negativity in other areas."

It was in her support group that Gail opened up for the first time about her celibate lifestyle. "Saying it aloud was empowering. I hadn't been much of a risk-taker, but with the encouragement of friends and later my therapist, I was able to begin standing up to Marc and taking control of my life."

Once you have worked with the test and scale above, you will have a better idea of the type of help you need. For Diana, relief from depression came from a combination of individual therapy and medication. Talking to a therapist can help with many kinds of depression, but talk therapy alone will not alleviate a depression as serious, pervasive, and biologically based as Diana's.

Diana recalls, "Dying was starting to look more appealing than living, and when I realized I had even created a plan as to how I might commit suicide, I became really frightened. I knew that I was in serious trouble and needed help quickly. Thankfully, the doctor I called saw me promptly. As he heard some of the details of my life, my M.D. explained that the continuing stress of living in a painful marriage affects all systems in the body, including the brain, and even slight changes in brain chemistry can cause depression. I now understood the physiological basis of my depression and why medication was necessary. He prescribed one of the newer antidepressants. This was a miracle drug for me. I now slept well and had energy. Within two weeks I was feeling much better, and a month later it was hard to believe that I had once come so close to getting out of my celibate marriage—permanently and in such a drastic way! Once the depression lifted I could think clearly and make concrete plans for leaving the marriage, and life's problems seemed manageable instead of overwhelming."

Therein lies the key. Overcome depression first, then decide what to do about your celibate marriage.

PUT YOURSELF FIRST

While you are working through your depression, you can make it easier on yourself by incorporating the following suggestions into your daily life. These things will give you more energy, lift your spirits, and generally help you to feel better.

1. Do not feel guilty about being depressed. It isn't your fault. You are not a failure as a wife or a woman. You need to accept the fact that you have done the best job you could with your own situation and circumstances.
2. Take good care of yourself physically. This will help you win

your battle against depression. Eat a healthy diet. Try to avoid sugary things, fried foods, and too much caffeine. Focus on whole grains, fruits, vegetables, and small servings of lean meat, poultry, and fish. Don't even think about going on any kind of strenuous, quick weight-loss diet, which might seriously aggravate your depression.

Avoid alcohol and drugs, for although they may make you feel a little better temporarily, they will make your depression worse. Many people do not know that alcohol is a depressant.

Exercise moderately. Many women notice a big improvement in their depression when they start a program of regular exercise, even as simple as a brisk 20-minute walk three times a week.

3. Do something nice for yourself at least twice a week. Plan these treats in advance, and don't let them get lost in the shuffle of family, work, and community responsibilities. Your health right now is a very important priority.

Ask yourself what might bring you pleasure and make you feel good. Here are some suggestions that have been helpful to some of the women we interviewed: a massage, a walk in the woods, a half-hour bubble bath with no interruptions, window-shopping at a mall, lunch with a good friend, time set aside for a favorite hobby, or an afternoon at the beach or by a lake. This list is really endless. Do whatever appeals to you.

Once you conquer depression, you free up the energy you put into being depressed. You can then direct this energy toward confronting the reality of your situation and coming to a considered decision. Although you may have been beaten down by depression, you still have the ability to make good choices and the power to rise to the challenges in your celibate life. In overcoming depression you take back your self and you recover the competent, capable decision-maker you are.

CHAPTER 5

DECIDING TO WORK ON YOUR SEX LIFE

* SAMANTHA
We make appointments for sex and have an agreement to respond to a request for sex within three days.

* SANDY
Thank God Bill went for treatment and his impotency was only temporary.

* MARJORIE
Stress is amenable to therapy and we were able to make changes which brought our sex life back into balance.

A job loss, a move, an illness, or a death—none of us is immune to the effect of such life events. Our lives can easily careen out of balance. Even one of life's most intimate aspects, sexuality, can tumble from high priority to low—sometimes, as with these celibate wives, to zero.

- Iris and Ben have lived in stony silence without sex since the death of their 17-year-old daughter in a car wreck four months ago.
- Hilda, at 45, is depressed and angry and cannot seem to adjust to living in yet another new city. She has been saying no to sex for six weeks.
- Laura's husband, Mike, has been job-hunting for 10 months. They are financially strapped, tense, irritable, and worried, and sex is the last thing on their minds.
- Sex took a nose dive when Sue's husband, Charles, started taking medication for high blood pressure.

Do you see your marriage reflected in any of the scenes above? As events in your life (over which you feel you have little or no control) change, the way you and your husband relate to each other may change; your sexual pleasure may diminish. You may wonder whether you are slipping into a permanently celibate marriage.

It is not unusual for patterns of sexual activity to change

103

over the lifetime of a marriage; they may be drastically altered at times of personal or family crisis. Stories of couples like those above are all too common. Pleasure, especially sexual pleasure, is easily relegated to the back burner when hearts and minds are burdened with feelings brought about by such events as the death of a loved one, financial insecurity, family difficulties, loss of a job, or medical problems. Most often short-term celibacy is a by-product of such situations, which place inordinate stress and anxiety on a couple.

Each of the women above is a victim of what is known as situational *Inhibited Sexual Desire* (ISD), the psychological term for an often complex problem manifested as the loss or lack of interest in sex as a result of some stressful life situation. Sex therapists tell us that loss of sexual desire is the most common complaint of their clients. But don't become discouraged as you read this. Situational ISD is often reversible when caring couples can communicate well and are able to uncover the underlying reasons. Working together, often with the help of a therapist, they can make the changes necessary to reduce the stressors that discourage intimacy and to reawaken love and desire.

"Putting the sizzle back into sex" is a popular media concept often made to sound easy. Don't be fooled into believing that reviving sex in your marriage can be accomplished easily or quickly. It is usually not as simple as catchy headlines would have you think. Magazine articles lead women to believe they can single-handedly create sexual fireworks in their marriages, and that will solve their celibacy problem. Don't fall into this trap, for the reality is that no matter how much you want sex back in your marriage, no matter how many self-help books you read, how much sexy lingerie you wear, how much weight you lose, or how many therapists you turn to, if your spouse is not interested you will only sink deeper into a pit of frustration, anger, and self-doubt.

But, if you and your spouse are *both* willing to invest your energies in regenerating your relationship and restoring good sex, we are optimistic that working together, with patience and commitment, you can achieve this highly desirable solution.

In this chapter we are dealing with marriages in which celibacy is fairly short-term or intermittent rather than a pattern firmly established over the years. However, even if you are coping with long-term celibacy, examining the conditions presented below will give you a broader view of the wide variety of situations that can impact negatively on your sex life. If you are a short-term celibate wife, you can begin to assess the quality of your overall relationship in order to determine if you, as a couple, have the prerequisites for sexualizing your marriage again. Long-term celibate wives too will find it useful to review their relationship with their spouses and gain a better understanding of what went wrong.

The following four conditions are the key relationship factors that offer the greatest possibility for a renewal of sex:

1. when the underlying cause of ISD is rooted in a life situation such as work-related stress, a move, concerns about aging, lives too tightly scheduled, a job loss, and so on
2. when the marriage is basically stable and sex has been generally satisfactory in the past
3. when there is good will between the partners and both have a strong desire to enjoy sex with each other again
4. when the couple can communicate on a deep and meaningful level with each other

Each of these factors will be explored in greater detail in the following pages, beginning with situational ISD.

AN INHIBITING SITUATION

When you find yourself having less or no sexual interest in each other and anxious weeks or months go by without sex, you and your spouse are most likely experiencing ISD. Although you may believe that celibacy is the problem in your marriage, it is really a symptom of some other condition in your relationship or life. Your ability to revive sex has a lot to do with what caused the problem.

Although ISD can be rooted in deep-seated psychological problems such as fear of intimacy or childhood abuse, or in physiological causes such as hormonal imbalances, our main concern is with circumstantial causes.

Situational ISD means exactly what it says: diminishing sexual desire as a result of one or more life events. Sometimes as we look back over the last year or two of our marriage, we fail to recognize how many stressful events have drained our energy and contributed to our disappearing interest in sex. Even in reportedly good marriages, stress is often the culprit, whether internal (worrying about getting older, for example, or being depressed) or external (such as work stress or an unwanted move). When several or many life events occur within too close a period of time, the accumulated stress chips away at both physical health and emotional well-being. A man may be alarmed to find himself impotent; a woman may feel so fatigued that she has no interest in sex.

The list below was inspired by the Holmes and Rahe scale designed to measure stress. As you read the list, make note of how many of these stability-disrupting situations have happened to you or your husband in the past year:

The death of a close family member
The death of a close friend

Serious illness in the immediate family

Losing a job or having work hours cut drastically

Losing an expected raise or promotion

Getting a promotion and expanding your work hours

Moving to a new town or city

Being the victim of a natural disaster such as a fire, flood, or hurricane

Credit card debt of over $5,000

Serious financial problems

Having a family member move in with you

The birth or adoption of a child

Being involved in a lawsuit

Having a family member arrested or jailed

Facing a problem with some type of addiction, whether your own or a family member's

Having trouble with rebellious teenagers

Being responsible for the care of elderly parents

Being in serious conflict with neighbors

A family member being seriously depressed or diagnosed with a mental illness

A sharp increase in the number of disagreements between spouses

A husband discovering he is impotent

Experiencing a midlife crisis

The wedding of your child

Every one of these situations, happy or unhappy, will bring a measure of stress and turmoil into your life. The greater the number of these events affecting your life in the past year, the higher the probability that you have felt overwhelmed by powerful feelings such as fear, guilt, anger, inadequacy, insecurity, and anxiety. These emotions can so consume your thoughts that the sensual images needed to stimulate sexual desires have been literally wiped out of your mind, until you find yourself wearily wondering when was the last time you had sex. Sex is mental before it is physical; it begins in your mind with images, remembered sexual experiences, and perhaps fantasies. It is almost impossible to feel relaxed, playful, sexy, and truly interested in your partner when you are stressed out and overwhelmed by your responsibilities. Sometimes we forget that our most important sex organ lies between our ears.

Many husbands and wives today are so stressed out and time-pressured that much of the pleasure, including sex, has gone out of their lives. It is important for you to consider the ways your life is being eroded by the tensions and pressures inherent in certain life events, for by identifying and understanding the impact of these events, you can set about to make changes.

Marjorie and David are typical of the many couples who must deal with situations forced on them by major life changes. In a little over a year, David's father had died suddenly, his mother had come to live with them, and Marjorie's hours as a legal secretary had been cut in half. David was a pilot for an international airline and was often away from home. Marjorie was left to cope with settling the paperwork on his father's affairs, closing up his parents' townhouse, and moving David's mother into their home. David's mother was devastated by her husband's sudden stroke and death and could not seem to manage even simple tasks. David was depressed when he was home, and Marjorie felt exhausted and resentful.

In the past they had used sex to comfort each other and relax, but David had little interest in sex now. When they did attempt it, Marjorie found that she was unable to let go and reach orgasm with her mother-in-law sleeping in the next room.

After a few weeks they gave up trying. They had been celibate for three months when Marjorie broke down in tears after a friend asked her how things were going. She poured out her frustrations and fears about her marriage. Over coffee the friend suggested that Marjorie see a therapist who had helped the friend through a divorce. Feeling desperate, Marjorie called and made an appointment for the next day.

Stress is amenable to therapy. Practicing relaxation techniques can immediately reduce stress, and viewing the problem more creatively, with the help of a therapist, can bring a sense of control. You can then take charge and make changes. Over the next several months the therapist helped David and Marjorie do just that. At David's suggestion his mother joined a bereavement support group and gradually started to seem more like her old self. During counseling David talked about losing his father and began to realize how much of a burden the death had placed on Marjorie.

They went away to a cozy bed-and-breakfast for a weekend. Here they were able to reestablish their sex life and make plans to look for another living arrangement for David's mother. Marjorie and David were functioning as a couple again and able to enjoy sex. Like teenagers, they planned trysts when his mother was out of the house; once they had sex in their car at the beach.

A death, a change in living arrangements, and a loss of income tore away the seams of Marjorie and David's sex life, but even if you have not had such stressful events in the past year you may still be severely stressed because of overcommitment to work or activities; serious, anxiety-producing time pressures; or a life spinning out of control. The following exercise will help you determine whether the stress you and your husband feel is responsible for your diminished sex life.

————————————————
It's All Too Much for Me

Number a page in your journal from 1 to 15 and write True next to the numbers corresponding to the statements below that you believe apply to you and/or your husband.

1. I do not feel secure in my job.
2. I feel overwhelmed by financial obligations.
3. We have put off major expenditures for fear of financial setbacks.
4. We do not take vacations except to visit family.
5. We rarely go out to a nice dinner or movie anymore.
6. I often feel there are not enough hours in the day.
7. I feel guilty because I don't spend more quality time with my spouse or children.
8. I fear that I'm losing touch with my friends.
9. I hardly ever get to spend time on hobbies or activities that used to bring me pleasure and satisfaction.
10. Sometimes I get angry that people make so many demands on me.
11. I often feel tired and unable to keep up with my hectic schedule.
12. I hardly ever feel sexy anymore.
13. My life feels out of control at times.
14. Sometimes I yearn for a return to a simpler, less complicated lifestyle.
15. I know I can't keep this pace up much longer.

If you have marked more than five statements true for you and/or your husband, it is time to make some changes in your life.

Samantha and Tom are an upwardly mobile, dual-career

couple. When their sex life ground to a halt, Samantha was working 60 hours a week as a corporate executive making twice the salary Tom earned. They realized upon reading this list that the cause of their diminished interest in sex could be traced to Samantha's overwork and overcommitment and the pressure Tom felt to expand his construction business and his income. Later in this chapter you will see how they turned the tables on celibacy and enjoyed sex again. Their process can serve as a model for changes you might choose to make in your life.

BUILDING ON A STRONG FOUNDATION

There is another crucial question to answer before you decide what steps to take to revive sex in your marriage. How well your marriage functions in terms of affection, understanding, and good communication will determine how far you can go in restoring the kind of atmosphere and cooperation needed to revitalize sex. You must ask yourself, "Do my husband and I have a good enough basic relationship to be optimistic about bringing the sizzle back into our sex life?" The following 15 qualities are strong indicators of a stable marriage.

EXERCISE ───────────────────────────────

Your Marriage—Rocky or Solid?

In your journal, number a page from 1 to 15. Mark True for those statements that describe your marriage.

1. My husband and I are good friends.
2. We share common interests and enjoy time spent with each other.

111

3. We respect each other and would never ridicule or degrade the other in public.
4. We are able to discuss and work out major issues such as finances and childrearing.
5. We share common goals and plans for our future.
6. After a disagreement, we are able to let go of our anger and do not hold grudges.
7. We make an effort to really listen to each other and feel heard and understood on major issues.
8. We are proud of each other's accomplishments.
9. We are affectionate; holding hands, hugging, and touching come naturally for us.
10. We make taking time with each other a priority in our life.
11. We agree that in the long run our relationship is more important than family or careers.
12. In the past we had a good sex life.
13. We understand that spouses are not mind readers, and we are comfortable asking for what we need for sexual fulfillment.
14. We are able to nurture ourselves and each other, understanding how important this is for both men and women.
15. Our love for each other is the glue that has held us together during difficult times.

If you answered True to most of these statements, it indicates that although something has gone awry in the relationship, you and your husband have a solid foundation on which to rebuild intimacy and sex in your marriage.

If most of your answers are no, your rocky marriage probably does not have the stable foundation needed to revive your sex life. You may want to consider other solutions to a celibate marriage, such as those other women share with us in chapter six (leaving) and chapter seven (staying).

Diana felt that her marriage lacked the stable foundation

for restoring a good sex life. She believed that her husband, though he might agree to go to counseling with her, had no intentions of changing.

"As I look back over my 26-year marriage, I understand that we did not have enough stability in our marriage to try to salvage our sex life. We were not really friends, we shared very few interests, we did not treat each other with respect, and we had not been able to work out everyday problems such as financial issues or questions about the children. We did not communicate effectively about everyday issues, and talking about making changes in our sex life raised feelings of inadequacy, anger, and suspicion."

Take time now to reflect on the basic strengths—or lack of them—in your marriage. You may spend minutes, hours, days, or weeks in this evaluation process. Don't rush it. You must believe strongly that your marriage is sound and worth saving before you approach your husband to discuss ideas for restoring good sex to your marriage. This may be one of the most important decisions you ever make, for if you try to rebuild your marriage and sex life on an unstable foundation, you may find yourself feeling like Diana. She recalls, "I was trying to do the impossible, fix the unfixable, when I could better have turned my energy into enjoying my children, building a career, and expanding my skills in golf, photography, and pottery."

WHERE THERE'S A WILL THERE'S A WAY

If you have decided that your marriage is basically sound and the potential exists for putting the sizzle back into sex, there is still another vital ingredient that can offer great hope—or sound the death knell to sexuality in your marriage. Since sex is not a solo act, *both you and your spouse* must vigorously reject celibacy and be willing to work together to reawaken your sex life. You need to know whether he is willing to participate with you in resexualizing your marriage.

If you cannot answer the following questions with a clear yes, the next step is to discuss your concerns with your spouse and try to obtain his cooperation.

My spouse will participate in whatever activity is necessary, for however long it takes, to reignite the spark in our sex life.

My spouse is willing to seek professional help with me.

My spouse is agreeable to trying new things or to changing old attitudes and behaviors.

Restoring our sex life is a top priority for us both.

Answering no to any of the statements above signals a flashing red light warning you that the chances for restoring sex with your husband are minimal and your goal probably unattainable, unless he can be persuaded of the necessity for his participation in the solution. A no also indicates that there may be deep-seated personal or interpersonal issues involved that could require intensive professional help (and, of course, a willingness to get this help).

Sandy and Bill are a perfect example of how quickly a marriage can fall apart when a husband refuses to acknowledge there is a problem and will not join his wife in seeking help. They had enjoyed an active sex life during the 19 years of their married life. Looking back, Sandy traced the beginning of their celibacy to one night when Bill couldn't get an erection. She wasn't worried—they'd been at a party and she thought Bill had had one too many. Bill was embarrassed and upset by the incident and brushed off Sandy's reassurances. When it happened the next week and the next, Bill shrank from Sandy's advances. She began to worry that she had done something to turn Bill off. They did not discuss this, and Sandy became angry and tried to convince herself that sex wasn't important anyway.

Bill's impotence was followed by depression, further undermining his self-confidence and ability to function at work as well as in bed. After three months of no sex and Bill's increasing depression, Sandy began to lose patience with him. "I turned into a shrew, bitching and complaining constantly. Everything Bill said or did annoyed me, and I let him know it too! I began to consider an affair or a divorce. I was desperate."

One afternoon Sandy turned on her favorite talk show and the subject was midlife impotence. She listened carefully as a doctor explained how common this problem is and that it can usually be treated successfully. Sandy felt elated and relieved to know there was help. She was astonished and angry when Bill refused to consult a doctor or to discuss their situation with a therapist.

Bill's reaction was not unusual. Many men find it very difficult to talk with anyone, even an M.D., about sexual problems. They often refuse to go for any type of treatment, as if admitting they need help makes them less of a man.

If you have asked, pleaded, or demanded that your husband go with you for help and he is unwilling to do so, there are several approaches you can take that we have seen work with couples. The first, if there is a medical problem, is for you to go ahead and make an appointment first with a physician and later, if needed, with a therapist. Sometimes saying, "We have an appointment to talk with Doctor so-and-so about our problem Tuesday at four o'clock" is enough to get your husband there. If you make the appointment and he refuses to go, go without him. You will probably gain insight and bring home information, perhaps pamphlets addressing the problem and listing local support groups. You have also broken the silence about your celibacy, and since the doctor knows about it already, your spouse may be less apprehensive about seeing the physician and talking about it.

Sandy pressured Bill, and eventually he did go to a urologist and was relieved to learn that there was no real physical cause for his impotence. The urologist referred them to a therapist experienced in dealing with the psychological causes of impotence. After several sessions of exploring Bill's midlife concerns about aging and his regrets about the roads not taken in life, their therapist suggested certain specific exercises (sensate focus, which we will discuss later). With this spur to sexual desire, Bill's impotence disappeared.

If your celibacy problem is not physical, but psychologically based, another method that is often successful is to make an appointment for yourself to discuss the matter with a therapist. Let your husband know that you will be going for this counseling once a week for a while. Husbands do not like to think their wives are talking about them with strangers without their input. Your husband may begin to wonder what you might be telling the therapist, and decide to have his side of the story heard. Tell your husband that he is welcome to join your sessions at any time. He may go out of curiosity, and then stay in therapy to work on the problem.

If your husband absolutely refuses to go with you for help, find your own therapist. You cannot bring back sex alone, and the time has come to examine your marriage closely to see if enough of your needs are being met to warrant staying in the relationship. Your therapist can help you answer such questions as, "What if I have an affair?" and "How important is sex to me?" as well as the ultimate question, "Should I consider separation or divorce?" Give yourself the gift of therapy. You have the right to ask for better communication; you have the right to ask for a sexually fulfilling life; you have the right to ask for outside help; you have the right to the best and happiest life possible.

Perhaps you have already discussed your celibacy concerns with your husband, and you feel certain that he is committed to working with you side-by-side to enjoy a good sex life again, and you have identified a high level of stability in your relationship. In this case you can expect to come to grips with the problem and reignite sex. Professional help may not be necessary. There are many things you and your husband can do to enhance your overall relationship and work toward setting the stage for renewed intimacy and sex. The story of Samantha and Tom may inspire ideas that you might wish to implement in your marriage.

Samantha and Tom believe in shared responsibility at home, with their children and for their relationship. Their marriage has survived its share of ups and downs; through periods of marital counseling they have honed their communication skills, and their relationship is honest and open.

When work-related stresses flattened their sex life, Samantha had been juggling triple roles as executive, wife, and mother. When they found themselves hostile and snapping at each other and their kids, they arranged for a baby-sitter and left home overnight to talk. Samantha fumed about her new hard-driving boss and the difficult project he had assigned her. She couldn't leave her worries at the office and was exhausted. Tom, a contractor, had taken on too many jobs and felt financially burdened and time-pressured. Sex, which had always been satisfying and a source of intimacy for them, suddenly seemed like too much trouble. Weeks and months went by without it. Now they were victims of inhibited sexual desire.

Because they live in a committed and loving relationship and because of former marital therapy, they knew how to listen and respond to each other in a clear, honest, and loving manner. They developed a system for doing their own interventions on behalf of their sex life. Their solutions, which took several months to work out, included spending time alone with each of their children and taking turns preparing meals. Tom was able to work through his need to compete with Samantha as the higher wage earner. They determined that bigger was not necessarily better, and since Samantha's career demanded travel, Tom determined that it was more important to cut back the number of jobs he said yes to and take on the role of PTA parent and Boy Scout leader for their three sons.

Samantha told us, "I now stop off at the Y several times a week to swim in order to unwind and rejuvenate myself before coming home after a harried workday. I started yoga and find it helps me to clear my head of work problems. We plan surprises for each other now and then. One time, Tom had my secretary block out time for a meeting. Then he picked me up and off we went for a hot-air balloon ride and a nice, relaxing dinner alone. Another time I arranged for a relative to keep the kids and I 'kidnapped' Tom and took him to a beachside motel for the weekend.

"We feel comfortable making appointments for sex, and if one of us is excessively tired, we agree that within a three-day period we will approach the other to have sex.

"We set aside five hours of every week that we spend alone together, and we have a rule that whenever we go out alone, like to a movie or dinner, we never talk about work issues or the kids."

Because Samantha and Tom have a basically solid happy marriage, communicate well, and are willing to work together to find solutions, and because their celibacy was a result of work-related situations creating intense pressure in their lives, they have been able to examine and change their harried lives. Now sex is a priority, an important part of their reorganized lifestyle.

It was clear to us, as Samantha described the efforts she and Tom make to keep their loving and sexual relationship flourishing, that they literally work at their marriage. This is important for all couples; good marriages don't just happen, they take work by both partners. This may sound unromantic, but evaluating, planning, communicating, and scheduling meetings are essential if a marriage is to thrive in today's stress-ridden times. Are you willing to work as hard at your marriage as you would at a job you wanted to keep?

BETTER LISTENING, BETTER LOVING

Having taken a measure of your relationship, let us assume that your celibacy is related to a difficult life situation, your marriage is stable, and your husband is as concerned and eager to share the pleasures of sex again as you are. However, you still have a problem: You find it hard to talk to him about your concerns. You may have bottled-up fears, old hurts, or feelings of self-consciousness that block you and your partner's ability to reach out to each other.

Learning to communicate better is a necessary precursor to rekindling both intimacy and sex in your marriage. Samantha and Tom had not started married life with great communication skills. In the early years of their marriage, following the birth of their children and while Samantha steadily climbed the career ladder, they turned to therapy to deal with their almost uncon-

119

trollable anger and fighting. Their therapist taught them how to listen and talk to each other. At first they felt awkward practicing the new skills in the therapist's office.

Tom had this to say to Samantha about time: "You spend practically no time with me and the kids. At night we have to compete with the damned phone when you spend hours talking to your mother."

Samantha at first felt attacked, but when she really listened for the feelings behind his words, she realized Tom felt neglected and lonely. She had not wanted to lay her problems on Tom every night so she ventilated them to her mother.

"I'm sorry, Tom," she replied. "I hate to dump on you and that's why I talk to Mom."

"Feel free to dump on me," Tom said. "I would rather know what's going on and feel a part of your life than walk around the house feeling angry while you're on the phone."

Samantha agreed to limit her calls to her mother to two nights a week. They set aside talk time for themselves, which meant scheduling a specific bedtime for the boys rather than the haphazard approach they had been using. The communication skills they had mastered provided a foundation for the good communication they practiced when sex became a problem.

You may not realize how important listening well is to communication. How well do you listen? When someone is talking, is your mind racing ahead, paying no attention to what the other person is saying? Do you find that you are waiting to refute, advise, instruct, or show how wise or clever you are? If so, step one is learning to listen carefully and patiently in order to let the other person know that you understand him. The following exercise will further clarify how you can share your own feelings and understand your partner's feelings.

EXERCISE
The Feelings Behind the Words

You and your spouse must agree to allow uninterrupted time for this exercise. Choose a private place. Your goal is to hear and understand what your partner is saying, feeling, and thinking, and you do this by trying to put yourself in his place. It will prove helpful if you can acknowledge to yourself that your opinion is merely your opinion and not a fact.

When you first begin to do this exercise, select topics that are less emotionally charged than sex until you are both comfortable talking with each other in this caring and nonthreatening way.

As your partner is speaking, do not allow yourself to get hooked into old reactions or allow your personal feelings to pull your attention away from what he is saying. Relax and look directly at him. Lean forward to indicate you are interested in him and what he is saying. Do not interrupt him. Ask yourself, "How would I feel if I saw it his way?"

Joan shares a recent situation between her husband and herself. "We moved into a new house, and my husband often came into the house with dirty shoes and tracked dirt on the carpet and tile floors. We have a mud room, but he kept forgetting to use it. My first reaction was to fume and yell at him while cleaning up the mess. I had to breathe deeply and back off. Then I asked him to sit down with me for a few minutes.

" 'I am trying to understand why, when we have a mud room, you cannot come in there and take off your shoes,' I told him. I continued, 'It makes me very angry. I feel used and put upon, and I cannot help wondering if you are angry about something and deliberately trying to upset me when you come in and dirty the rugs.'

121

"My husband replied, 'No, I'm really not trying to upset you. It's a big hassle to sit down and take my shoes off and then put them on again when I go out. It's really just laziness.'

"I replied, 'I appreciate your honesty. Yes, I can see where that could be a bother. But after a while the dirt isn't going to come out of the carpet. Would it help if I put a sign on the front door to remind you to use the mud room?'

"He agreed to that and has made a conscious effort to remove his shoes ever since. My husband heard me. He did not feel attacked, and he didn't ignore me as he had when I was yelling and angry at him. He explained his reasons, and I understood his feelings as he did mine."

In working through an issue, you don't have to reach an agreement, but you do have to reach a compromise that satisfies both of you. This process really works and can seem miraculous, for it breaks down barriers and opens the door to understanding and trust.

When you dialogue in this tactful and nonthreatening manner about nonsexual issues, you will become more comfortable saying what's on your mind concerning sex. For example, you might say, "I am upset that we have not had sex for weeks now. I'm not sure if you are angry with me or what, and I feel very nervous about approaching you. I feel hurt and rejected."

Note that you have only told your partner how you feel. You have not demanded anything from him or accused him of anything.

Another approach might be, "It worries me that neither of us seems to have the energy or interest in sex. I miss sex with you. Let's talk about it and see if we can't get it started again. It would mean a lot to me if we could work this out."

It is ironic that after years of so-called sexual freedom, sexual straight talk is still hard to come by for many couples, when we know that good communication is very important for a happy relationship. Good communication softens the hurt and washes away angry emotions. It warms your heart toward your spouse and leads to feelings of compassion, confidence, and intimacy. When you can broach sensitive subjects, clear up old issues, and get more of the understanding and love you crave, you increase the chances for ending short-term celibacy in your marriage.

We have adapted the following exercise that was designed by sex researchers William Masters and Virginia Johnson as the first step in an arousal technique for couples in sex therapy. Known as sensate focus 1, the idea is for a couple to take turns exploring each other's bodies by massage and touching. In this exercise the couple is instructed not to touch each other's genitals (including breasts) and not to have intercourse, in order to relieve the pressure to perform and in order to create a nonthreatening atmosphere in which they can relax and safely tell each other what pleases and does not please them.

If you can relax and enjoy doing this sensate focus exercise, not only will it help transform sex from dull to delicious, it will enable you to share sexual feelings with your spouse about what arouses you and where and how you like to be touched. Another advantage is that it can be done whenever one partner feels a need for touching and stroking; it addresses the oft-heard complaint from women, "He never touches me unless he wants intercourse."

Fred Shotz, researcher, sex educator, and therapist in Fort Lauderdale, Florida, cautions that some people may find this exercise boring or irritating. Should this be the case for you or your husband, do not try to force your partner to do this.

Bill and Sandy entered into this exercise with relish. It proved to be very effective in removing the obstacles that made

Bill impotent, and it also proved to be an open sesame for talking about sex.

EXERCISE

Getting the Love You Crave

Agree with your partner that each of you will spend about a half hour (or longer) touching, stroking, and caressing the other without touching the genitals or having intercourse.

Together, select a massage cream or lotion that is of a consistency and odor pleasant to both of you. Choose a very private place where you will not be interrupted. Decide who will go first. Your partner may find it easier to begin by massaging your feet, then moving gently upward (avoiding your breasts) as he caresses your body slowly. Relax and allow yourself to receive (and later to give him) pleasure. As there is no pressure to have intercourse, this is the time for each of you to focus on your own erotic places and your pleasure and to tell your partner exactly what turns you on or off.

If this was pleasurable, you might want to go on to sensate focus 2, in which a couple is instructed to touch each other's genitals but to treat these parts with no more attention than any other. At another time you could move on to touching each other's genitals with your hand on his, and then vice versa, to guide and direct the placement and pressure of touch. By then you should have established trust and a rapport for sharing your sexual likes and dislikes with each other.

After using the sensate focus exercises several times, it might be easier to talk about reading erotic books, watching X-rated films, trying new positions, or even semi-public sex, such as sex on the beach or in a park behind a fountain. Excitement is heightened by the possibility of discovery. The old cliché that says variety is the spice of life can be given new meaning by a loving couple trying new things. With love, tenderness, imagination, playfulness, and joy, you too can bring the sizzle back to sex.

Dr. Shotz encourages couples to make sex fun. "When we become adults things we did as kids that were play are now work, like bike riding. It used to be fun, but now, for some of us, it's exercise. As adults we can use our sexuality to play with the person we love." Sensate focus can help a couple learn to play as well as love again.

Samantha and Tom read about sensate focus and decided to give it a try. They were delighted with the results. Samantha told us, "What a great way to just relax and be able to finally tell Tom what I preferred when we fooled around. We ended up feeling very close and loving, and we use it whenever we need to give sex a special boost."

When you begin to talk more freely about your sexual desires and needs with your spouse, remember to accent the positive. It is much easier for your partner to hear "I love it when you nibble on my ear and lick my neck" than, "I can't stand it when you pinch my nipples." Concentrate on communicating what you like and want more of during sex. Take your partner's hand and show him the areas that are most arousing for you. Making love noises can indicate your pleasure and serve to increase your partner's arousal. Some couples find using "dirty words" arousing, while others prefer talking about how much they love each other. Let your partner know what pleases you. Be willing to be genuinely interested in what turns him on and to try things he might suggest. Be open and honest about how you feel, and don't be coerced into doing anything that frightens or upsets you. Good sex means anything that *both* partners enjoy.

We do not want to hold out false hope for bringing sex back into your bedroom. However, we have seen many happy and satisfied women report their success at resexualizing their marriages in cases of short-term celibacy. In each situation they evaluated their marriages as stable, their husbands as caring and cooperative, and they had upgraded their communication skills when necessary. Such a marital picture offers the best opportunity for putting an end to unwanted celibacy.

Maybe, like Samantha and Tom, who are skilled at communicating with each other, you might be able to restore sex in your marriage without professional help. However, many couples are best served by seeking the aid of a sex therapist.

WHAT CAN A THERAPIST DO FOR YOU?

A therapist can help you evaluate your relationship. In therapy you may see for the first time the emotional games you are playing with each other. You may learn things that each of you does that make closeness and good sex difficult.

A therapist can help you communicate with your spouse. You may learn ways in which one or both of you is sabotaging communication by interrupting, changing the subject in mid-conversation, accusing, blaming, or using gestures like finger pointing that make good communication almost impossible.

A therapist can help you deal with conflict. You can learn how to fight without holding on to grudges or hitting below the belt. You can accomplish more by waiting until you've calmed down and then using an "I" message. For example, "I feel insignificant and unloved, and this makes me angry when I can't get your attention to discuss things that are important to me," rather than barking with an angry edge in your voice, "Dammit, you're so selfish. Why don't you put that paper down and listen to me?"

A therapist can provide you with sexual information that will allow you to expand your sexual repertoire. A potpourri of information, tools, and techniques has flooded the sex therapy field in the last few years, such as the beautifully presented, erotic, and educational *Better Sex Video Series,* written and narrated by Fred Shotz; as well as fully and frankly illustrated sex manuals like *Sexual Happiness for Women,* by Maurice Yaffe, Elizabeth Fenwick, and Raymond Rosen, designed to heighten your sexual awareness.

How Do You Find a Therapist?

The Appendix at the end of this book offers advice on finding a therapist. It is advisable to shop for the right therapist, and the process can be very confusing, for professional counselors come with a variety of titles. There are psychiatrists (medical doctors), psychologists (designated "Ph.D."), and master's level therapists and social workers. Studies have shown that the personality of the therapist and how you relate to that person is as important as his or her title or school of therapy. If you like and trust the therapist, chances are you will accept and benefit from his or her methods.

Many people ask friends for references when they are considering using a therapist for marital or other problems. In the case of a celibate marriage, however, many women have never told anyone about the problem, not even their closest friend. It is unlikely that you will want to tell people you are living a celibate life and need someone to help you change that.

In contacting therapists, do not be afraid to ask questions.

You are the consumer and you do not have to stand in awe of therapists. Bringing sex back into your marriage will most likely require the help of someone skilled both in psychological and sex therapy. You need to ask the following questions:

"Are you specifically trained in sex therapy?"
"Do you have experience working with couples dealing with short-term celibacy?"
"Have you been successful in helping couples bring sex back into their marriages?"

Is-This-Therapist-the-Right-One-for-Us-Checklist

Here are some points to consider in determining if a therapist is the right person for you to be working with. After four to six sessions, ask yourself,

Are you comfortable with the therapist and able to discuss your most intimate issues?
Do you feel that the therapist is fair to both you and your spouse and does not take sides?
Are you beginning to see specific positive changes in your relationship and behavior?
Does your therapist always keep your relationship on a professional basis?

This last point means that your life and that of the therapist are kept separate. You may feel flattered and special if your therapist takes a personal interest in you, but it was disastrous for one woman when her therapist assumed the role of surrogate mother, advising her whom to marry, attending the wedding, and encouraging her to stay married when she was very unhappy.

The woman felt guilty and then outraged when, unable to resolve her celibacy, she finally decided to divorce her husband.

If you cannot answer yes to the questions above, you might bring them up in a therapy session for discussion. If you are not satisfied with the answers, you might start to look for another therapist.

Whether you and your husband seek the help of a therapist, or together attempt to put an end to your celibacy without a therapist, it is the goal that is important, not how you get there. Reinventing your sex life can be frustrating and difficult, but as sexual interest and feelings begin to return and you are able to enjoy this aspect of your relationship again, your marriage in all probability will be stronger and happier than it was before. You cannot put so much effort into examining your life, and perhaps in learning to talk to each other in a new way, without growing in self-awareness and self-confidence.

It is our wish for you that you have indeed been able to reawaken passion and have come full circle from the sad loneliness of celibacy to the joy and fulfillment of renewed sexuality.

CHAPTER 6

DECIDING TO LEAVE

✳ STEPHANIE
After we married I felt no sexual attraction for my husband, yet
unhappy as I was, I didn't file for divorce until our daughter was six
years old. I had no idea then that I had been sexually molested when
I was six; I only knew that there was an anxiety and intense pressure
inside of me to leave the marriage.

✳ JANE
I was terrified to be alone, and it took me years of celibacy, drinking
too much, and feeling devastated living in the shadow of his mistress
before life became so unbearable I could no longer avoid filing for
divorce.

✳ DIANA
Even though I'd made the choice to leave my marriage, I was faced
with the difficult decision of how to handle sex in this day of AIDS.

Reading about couples who were able to reawaken sex in their marriages, you may have felt discouraged about your own situation or envious of women whose husbands were willing to work with them to solve their celibacy problem. You may still be struggling to accept the fact that you cannot change your husband or to accept celibacy as a permanent part of your life. Don't despair, there are other answers to a celibate marriage.

If you are to lead a satisfying and happy life, it may be necessary for you to leave your marriage. Deciding to leave can be one of the most difficult choices you have to make, and by the time you make this decision you may have spent many years longing for what might have been, hoping for change, weeping for lost joys, feeling anxious about lifestyle changes and how divorce might affect your children. During all this time you have probably vacillated between staying and leaving. Both of the authors shared this experience, swearing to get out and then retreating from the decision to leave their marriages.

Joan made several fruitless attempts to seek divorce. "After about eight years of continual conflict over sex, I felt that I had to get out of my marriage," she explains. "The first attorney I visited stressed all the difficulties of obtaining a divorce in the state I lived in. He provided the excuse I needed to stay put, for at the same time I was discussing divorce there was a huge lump in my throat and I was filled with sheer terror. I backed off the issue of divorce and settled for several more years of bickering over sex and living through gaps of celibacy.

"I separated from my husband a few years later, but under pressure from my family and children and my own inability to stand on my own two feet I recapitulated, returned, and stayed two more years. I was stuck in the belief, which many women have, that I should always be taken care of or rescued by someone else. I was afraid to divorce without having another man on whom I could load my dependency."

Diana faced her own repertoire of insecurities. She recalls, "Unhappy as I was, it took me seven years from the time I saw the first attorney until I was able to get out of my marriage. The attorney was brutally realistic about my financial situation, reminding me that I had no rich parents to pick up the pieces, I had no boyfriend waiting in the wings to support me and my children, and my husband had a history of not paying his bills. He urged me 'if at all possible' to stay in the marriage until my children were out of school. Three years later, when all but one of the kids were out of high school, I did move out, for nine months. Ned asked me to return, professed his undying love, and agreed to go for couples counseling. We went to a marriage encounter weekend and I believed this was a breakthrough in our relationship, for we were able to talk with each other at a new level of intimacy. We came home with a framework for continued sharing of feelings, but by Monday noon it was as if it had never happened. I was back in the marriage and nothing had changed."

When you finally make a decision and are no longer torn with doubt, you give your life direction. If you have no clear vision of what you want or where you want to go, you will most assuredly find yourself walking along in someone else's tracks, taking a path you would not have chosen for yourself. You will be living someone else's agenda. If this is how you have been living, you probably feel unfulfilled, dissatisfied, and unhappy. We know from experience that you will feel even more so unless you take responsibility for living your own life.

Jane is a perfect example of a woman who, by not deciding, subjected herself to the dictates of her husband, setting herself up for seven years of sexual rejection and celibacy as she tried to cope with his infidelity.

Jane and Leo had lived a lavish, hedonistic lifestyle, which included an active sex life for 14 years, until their colicky and demanding son was born when Jane was 40. Self-centered and inflexible, Leo continued to expect the same degree of attention and companionship, which Jane, ill and exhausted, was unable to provide. Within a few months Jane felt abandoned when Leo spent frequent nights away from home and betrayed when she discovered that he had a lover.

Jane recalled a particularly painful moment. "One night at dinner he simply announced he didn't want to have sex with me anymore. I cried and begged and tried to seduce him even while he smelled of another woman's perfume. Nothing worked. I'd come from a poor family and the idea of raising Jason alone and supporting myself was terrifying. I wanted to curl up in a corner and die."

Leo went about living his own life and Jane went on focusing on Jason. At night she drank to dull her pain and to avoid the necessity of making any decision.

Then the family moved to Canada. Jane felt disoriented and displaced in a new town. Jason started first grade. Frustration, loneliness, and concern about her drinking sent Jane into counseling, where she began to answer the questions, Who am I? What do I want and how can I get it? How can I find the strength to get out of my miserable, celibate marriage?

It took Jane eight months of therapy to realize that she was an emotionally abused wife as well as a sexually deprived one. That was when she began to work through her years of suppressed anger. Her therapist also encouraged her to upgrade her secretarial skills by becoming proficient on the computer. With much anxiety, Jane enrolled at the community college and became so swift and capable at this new technology that she was offered a job with a large company in another city. Still leery about being a single parent, Jane might have turned it down, again deciding not to decide, had Leo not brought his mistress to Canada and set her up in an apartment down the street from their house. This was the final indignity. Jane had gained enough self-confidence not to accept such degrading treatment any longer. Seven years almost to the day after Jason was born, she filed for divorce, accepted the job offer, and moved with her son to another city.

Life has not always been easy for Jane, but at 60 she is enrolled in college with the goal of becoming a journalist. We wish her well.

No One Should Live Like This

Jane had time to make her decision to leave, upgrade her skills, and find a job before she filed for divorce. But you may not have the option of a leisurely decision-making process. In the case of physical abuse, you need to leave as soon as possible. Physical abuse demands that you act immediately to get out of a situation where you and your children are threatened with bodily harm. Your husband's behavior will not change and will probably become more violent with time. Remember the horrifying FBI statistics that every 15 seconds a woman is battered and every 6 hours a woman dies at the hands of her husband. Get out now. No one should live like this. We urge you to pick up a phone and contact your local crisis center or United Way office, which can provide you with the number of a local shelter for battered women, or you may call the National Domestic Violence Hotline at 1-800-333-7233.

There are other situations that are particularly emotionally damaging for celibate wives. If you see your life reflected below, we counsel you to seek help immediately. The status quo is destructive to you and your children. Many women do not label verbal lashings as abuse, but as Beverly Engel warns us in *The Emotionally Abused Woman*, "Abuse is any behavior that is designed to control or subjugate another human being through fear, humiliation, and verbal and physical assaults." If you are married to an emotionally (verbally) abusive husband, recognize that you both have a problem. Your husband is a person with low self-esteem who feels superior when he is in control, while on an unconscious level you probably feel that you do not deserve any better. Stay and your self-esteem will plummet ever lower as you are continually devalued and criticized. Unless your partner is willing to acknowledge his behavior and work with you in counseling to make changes, you should seek help for yourself in order to gain the confidence you need to get out of your abusive marriage.

Another form of emotional abuse is practiced by the philanderer, a man who is repeatedly unfaithful. "What's wrong with me? Why does he want sex with other women?" you howl inside. A better question might be, "What's wrong with him?" Frank Pittman, in his groundbreaking study of infidelity, *Private Lies*, tells us that a philanderer's behavior "says little about you, his wife, and a lot about his own deep-seated fears and emotional problems, which you cannot solve." Pittman describes a philanderer as a man whose "primary emotion is anger." If the pain of being celibate while he is chasing other women is more than you can bear, make plans to get out of the marriage when it is most advantageous to you.

You probably haven't given much thought to the many ways your celibacy has affected various areas of your life. There are probably things you do or say, some of which you are not even aware of, that have a detrimental impact on your children or yourself.

Taking anger and frustration out on your children, for example, is abusive behavior that demands timely action. You may find yourself unintentionally slipping into verbal or physical abuse of your children. Screaming at them, "Damn you," or "Shut up," or criticizing, "You never do anything right," or "You're so stupid," is verbal abuse. Hitting, slapping, or shoving them is physical abuse. You are probably taking your anger at your husband out on your children. When you feel this anger building up, take time out. Get away from the children until you get yourself under control. Have a cup of tea or coffee, dig in the garden, sew, read a magazine, call a friend. Do something to divert your attention from your children. Many community mental health centers offer individual or group counseling for parents in this situation. You will find support if you call the Parents Anonymous National Hotline for information and referral, 1-800-775-1134.

Celibate wives may fall victim to self-destructive behavior that seems to ease the pain temporarily. You may find, for example, that the one glass of wine you enjoyed in the evening is now a bottle of wine every day. Or you may realize that you turn to the refrigerator whenever you feel sad, lonely, or frustrated. Or you frequently need pills to attain the oblivion of sleep.

In the following exercise, give serious consideration to the statements. Your responses will mirror behavior you may not be aware of. You need to take very seriously any statements you answer True.

EXERCISE ──────────────────────────────
How Has Celibacy Affected My Life?

Number a page in your journal from 1 to 16 and write True for every statement that applies to you.

1. My sexual frustration makes me irritable, and I often yell at, shove, or hit my children.
2. My behavior is often irrational, impulsive, or unreasonable.
3. I meet my sexual needs outside my marriage, and this satisfies me.
4. I meet my sexual needs outside my marriage, but this causes me further unhappiness.
5. I have become a compulsive shopper.
6. I have gained weight, eating out of frustration.
7. I am discouraged about myself as a woman and don't care how I look.
8. I make sure I look good and I flirt with men.
9. I feel keyed up and anxious all the time.
10. I am very critical and impatient with my children.
11. I ignore my children because I find their requests too demanding.
12. I am drinking more because it dulls the pain of staying in my marriage.
13. I treat my husband with cool indifference.
14. I can't sleep without pills or relax without tranquilizers.
15. I make jokes and try to give others the impression that sex is a hot item in my house.
16. I am very critical and impatient with my husband.

The more statements you have numbered True, the more urgently you need to seek help. These behaviors tell you that it is time to get your life under control. Almost every community offers self-help groups, such as one of the 12-step programs or weight-loss programs, which will offer support and guidance.

FIRST STEPS

This chapter deals with the considerations that go into deciding whether to leave your celibate marriage. However indecisive you are, however long you have been married, the time to begin to assume responsibility for your own life is right now, today. Step out of your husband's tracks and find your own pathway to happiness. Your strengths and your answers lie within yourself, waiting to be tapped.

As part of this process, we will look at how the people and events of your earliest years impact on your life today, and we will explore the issue of self-esteem and lead you through some steps to help you feel better about yourself.

But first it will be easier, and you can make a wiser and more reasoned choice, if you reflect seriously on the questions, What are the advantages and disadvantages of this marriage? How important is sex to me? What do I really want? What am I really afraid of, and how can I stop being so afraid? By defining and examining the positive and negative aspects of your marriage in the exercise below, you can gain deeper self-awareness and more clarity about what you really want. You may not come up with the "correct" answer right now, but you will have clarified your position and initiated the decision-making process.

EXERCISE

Why Stay, Why Leave?

In your journal, number 1 to 8 and list eight reasons for *staying* in your marriage. Below that, number 1 to 8 again and make a list of eight reasons for *leaving* your marriage. Select one reason from the staying list and, on a separate piece of paper, write at least a paragraph expanding on why this is a good reason for you to remain married. Then select one reason from the leaving list and do the same. Do not censor what you are writing. Write what is truly in your heart, how you really feel.

Take time to carefully consider each reason for staying or

leaving. Weigh the two lists against each other as if on a scale. Is there an obvious imbalance? Does the scale tip strongly toward staying or leaving?

You may need to write more paragraphs or pages about the reasons for staying or leaving your marriage to further refine your thinking and come to a more clearheaded decision.

Your celibacy will probably be on your list of reasons to leave. For Joan, however, the sexual constraints in her marriage seemed always to be counterbalanced by the positive aspects of her life with Neal. Joan's list of pros was long: Neal was her advocate, treated her royally, was a good provider, encouraged and was proud of her accomplishments, was supportive, loyal, kind, and honest, and a man who placed his family above anything else. Joan handled their financial affairs and played a major role in all decision-making. Joan says, "Even though celibacy weighted the scales heavily against the marriage, it took years before I could justify leaving, since I had been taught to value all these qualities in a man."

To help you determine if your unhappiness is due primarily to your celibacy or to other unsatisfactory aspects of your marriage, this chapter asks you to look at the way celibacy affects your marriage and all facets of your life. Is celibacy altering the way you eat, sleep, live, and treat your children? How does it affect the way you feel about yourself as a woman? Does it motivate you to have affairs or, conversely, to avoid men altogether because you feel you are too unattractive?

With these factors in mind, we go on to a most important question, How important is sex to you? Is it worth giving up the things you listed as reasons to stay? As you work with the emotionally charged issues involved, you will be examining in depth just how vital sex is in your life. This is a major consideration in helping you to decide if you need to make a change as drastic as divorce.

EXERCISE
How Important Is Sex to Me?

On a scale of 1 to 10, where would you rate sexual satisfaction in importance? We are referring here to your overall sexuality, so consider the three following aspects of sex in your decision: emotional intimacy, touching and holding, and the physical release of orgasm.

How Important Is Sex to Me?

1 -- 10
Of little   Very
importance   important

If you rate sex as high as an 8, 9, or 10, the unhappiness you feel from being deprived of sex might be enough reason to end your marriage and look for a new sex partner, especially if— and this is important—you identified many other disadvantages in evaluating the pros and cons of your marriage. Your list, for example, might include such items as: he gambles, he puts me down, he is unreliable, he lies, he cheats, he drinks, he's a lousy father. Coupled with the importance of sex, these are clear signals that you should be considering ending your marriage.

If you rated the importance of sex as only a 2 or a 3, you may be the type of woman who can forgo sexual activity for the rest of your life and not really miss it. There may be many other areas of your life that bring you happiness, and there may be compensations within the marriage worth staying for.

If you rated sex as a 5, 6, or 7, your decision may be more complicated. Sex is important to you but there are other aspects of your marriage that may be as important as, or more important than, your celibacy.

Diana tried for years to convince herself that she could live celibately. "I rationalized that I could live without sex and tried to fill my needs for touching and holding with regular massage appointments.

"Slowly I came to understand that the part of sexuality I missed most was the intimacy, that emotional openness and sharing which can take place when two people make love rather than just have sex. As it became clear that this would never again be a part of my marriage, I knew I would have to leave my marriage and seek this intimacy in another relationship."

Different women react to celibacy in different ways. You may stay so busy that you fall into bed at night too tired to think about sex. Or you may be so immobilized by depression that you aren't able to do much of anything. You may be a woman who is always irritable in sexual frustration.

EXERCISE

How Celibacy Affects My Life

Take a page or two in your journal to complete this statement: *Because of my celibacy I have become* . . .

Diana wrote, "I have become an underground sexual person. I don't dress, walk, or talk in sexy ways but feel that I am supressing a rich well of sexuality."

Joan wrote, "During my marriage I felt at times unrecognizable; sometimes calm and controlled, and sometimes filled with sexual urges that made me feel crazy and out of control."

143

Delving into your feelings, taking a hard look at the way you feel celibacy has affected your life and behavior, raises the question, Are you satisfied to go on living this way? This reality confronts you with your deepest feelings as you face the depth of your discontent. Yet this may still not be enough to move you out of the relationship, for first you need to understand who you are and what you want for your life.

MEMORIES

Having the courage to get out of a celibate marriage is not easy, even when you say, "I can't go on like this, I'm miserable, there must be something better." We will help you to use your memories to gain a clearer vision of who you are and what you want.

Our decision-making process is clouded by mistaken beliefs and attitudes we all grew up with. These beliefs tell us who we are, what the world is like, and how others should treat us. For example, you may believe that you are responsible for making your marriage work or that it is your fault your husband is not interested in sex, or you may believe that you have to settle for an unhappy life because you don't deserve any better. Your childhood, happy or sad, was where it all started. From your three- or four-foot-high perspective you interpreted the positive or negative situations that confronted you and laid the foundation for your belief system, which continues to prejudice and distort your judgment and decisions today.

Examining your childhood memories is an effective way to uncover the events that have shaped your personality and outlook on life and that underlie the way in which you handle your celibate marriage. Dr. Kevin Leman and Randy Carlson begin their insightful book, *Unlocking the Secrets of Your Childhood*

Memories, with this promise: "Tell us about your earliest child-hood memories and we'll tell you about yourself today." Retrieving and examining your early memories can help you explode outdated beliefs and clear the way for the very best of you to emerge.

You may be wondering why, out of the hundreds of incidents that occurred so long ago, you remember only a few. This is because these particular incidents are deeply etched in your memory. It may surprise you to realize that your early memories are astonishingly consistent with the person you are now.

Diana admitted that she had had an irrational fear that she would end up on the streets as a bag lady if she divorced. She wondered if this was some kind of precognition of her fate, and she worried that if she decided to divorce she might never be able to manage on her own financially. When she retrieved the following childhood memory, she was able to put her concerns in perspective with a sigh of relief.

When I was six I threatened to run away from home. My mother helped me pack six grocery bags of clothing, and though it was summer, she insisted I include my winter underwear. We carried my bags outside the front door, where she left me. We had a corner house and I pulled the bags as far as the curb, where I sat huddled among them, crying and in great distress, feeling terrified, unloved, and unwanted.

Long forgotten, this memory provided the basis for Diana's irrational fear of destitution on a street corner. Once she understood how these old feelings affected her ability to leave her marriage, Diana could say to herself, "Of course a six-year-old couldn't leave home successfully. I am an adult with skills and experience, and I can plan for the financial and emotional security I need in order to leave this relationship." That is just what she did.

I Remember . . . Now I Understand

Think back to your earliest memory. Focus on a specific event. For example, don't generalize, "My family made me feel special." Instead personalize, "I was about four and I remember dancing on the long, shiny dining room table while my parents and grandparents applauded."

You may have a memory on the tip of your tongue; perhaps you have told it to many people over the years. Or you may need to take some time to retrieve a recollection. Here are some memory joggers to help you:

Were you mostly sad or happy as a child?
How did you feel about your brothers and sisters?
What special events or holidays did you celebrate?
How did you feel about your parents and grandparents?
If there was a major life-changing event like divorce, illness, moving, death, or birth, how did it affect you?

In your journal write the memory that comes to you in its entirety, as if you were writing out a little story, as Diana did above. Tell your tale from an "I" perspective, and be sure to describe your feelings at the time of the event as clearly as you can recall them.

One woman, Louise, recalled, "When I was about seven, I enjoyed touching my vagina when I went to bed. It felt good. My mother came in one night and caught me. She called my father and they scolded me and slapped my hands. Terrified, humiliated, and in tears, I promised never to do that again." As a married woman, Louise did not enjoy foreplay and was eager to get sex over with. Her husband, Jim, justified his philandering by blaming Louise for their sex problems. In recalling her memory Louise gained insight into what was happening in her bedroom.

We hope you have an idea now how this process works. In your journal write down your memory.

I remember when I was _____

_____

_____

_____

When you are finished, reread your memory story. What is your story about? Is it about being sad, or fearful, or brave: losing trust in someone, or being applauded for something? Remember, your early memories relate directly to your present beliefs about life, so they may provide, as they did for Louise, a direct link to your attitudes about sex and marriage.

As you consider your early childhood memory, go deeper than a mere description of the event. Capture the meaning of your memory. How did the main character (you) in the story feel? Louise had been mortified and certain that touching herself (and later being touched) was disgusting and wrong. She then realized why she had rated the importance of sex in her life as very low. Seeking to save her marriage, and with the help of a sex therapist, Louise rejected her no-longer-useful child's perspective about sex. She forgave Jim his infidelities, and forgave her parents their ignorance. In time, as trust between Jim and Louise grew, she learned to relax and began to enjoy sex.

147

Spend some more time thinking about other childhood experiences. As you remember these events, ask yourself, "Are there any similarites in the way I felt in my memory and the way I feel now as an adult?" Do your memories help you to understand why you are afraid to leave or why you stay in your sexless marriage?

The following story is a perfect example of how an event, though unremembered for a long time, accounted for celibacy in a marriage.

Stephanie, now in her thirties, shared with us the way in which working with an early memory freed her to lead a more satisfying life. Stephanie's early memory of childhood sexual molestation lay buried in her unconscious and was retrieved through hypnosis after her divorce. The powerful, negative energy of this unremembered event had been the direct cause of her lack of sexual desire for her husband and of her celibacy.

"I married Frank and immediately lost all interest in sex with him," she told us. "Frank wanted sex all the time, and I used every excuse to put him off. Frank was an inconsistent provider. When his schemes and plans and the next new project didn't work, he blamed anyone but himself. I resented dipping into money I had saved to meet end-of-the-month expenses. He was not a strong, decisive man, and I lost all trust in him and respect for him. When I wanted to talk things out, he withdrew. I assumed these were the reasons I was turned off sexually."

When their daughter, Amanda, was born, Stephanie devoted herself to mothering but was still unhappy. She wanted to leave but she rationalized, "He's great with our daughter and he certainly never beats me or drinks or anything like that." By the time they had been married eight years and Amanda was six, Stephanie was becoming increasingly anxious and unhappy. "I knew I wanted a divorce," she admitted, "but I had never lived alone, and I was terrified that I couldn't make it on my own."

Then Stephanie took Amanda, without Frank, to her mother's for Thanksgiving dinner. She had never done anything without Frank before. Suddenly she felt a sense of power and strength. Stephanie continued to do things on her own and even started going back to college.

When she asked for a divorce, Frank was not cooperative. The divorce was drawn out and very unpleasant. Reeling from the stress of her divorce, Stephanie entered therapy and agreed to try hypnosis. Then began the painful recall of childhood sexual molestation.

When she was six Stephanie was hospitalized for head injuries from a bicycle accident. Her badly cut head was bandaged and her eyes covered. Her grandfather, whom she adored, stayed with her. Lying next to her in the bed and trying to soothe her with his touches, he began to fondle her body and genital area. Stephanie told us, "I had no conscious waking memory of this event. Under hypnosis I heard myself screaming, 'Get out of here, I want my Mommy,' but in reality I doubt if I really screamed at all. I would have been too afraid to do that—too afraid of losing the person I loved the most." So, like other childhood victims, Stephanie disassociated herself from the event. She did this by "forgetting" it. That repression led to her sexual numbness in marriage.

The puzzle of Stephanie's low sex drive and her inability to relax and get aroused with Frank fell into place. She now understood why she had turned off sexually to Frank as soon as he became a "family member." Stephanie also realized that she had filed for divorce when her daughter became six—the exact age when she had been molested. Subconsciously she believed she had to protect her daughter from a similar experience.

Confronting the past and gaining control over it helped Stephanie solve her problem.

Stephanie's story is more common than you might imagine. It is estimated that one of every three women are sexually molested at some time in their childhoods. Those women who marry may experience an inability to be intimate sexually, have unexplained nightmares, bouts of anxiety or panic attacks, depression, or stress-related disorders that are never diagnosed and earn them the label of hysteric or hypochondriac. Women have discovered that talking about the abuse is the way out of the trauma. Stephanie had a good listener in her therapist. Now happily remarried, as a therapist herself Stephanie leads groups for women who have been abused.

If you were abused in childhood, chances are there may be large blocks of your early years you cannot remember. You may also experience some of the symptoms mentioned above. If you are interested in investigating this area of your life, we would advise that retrieving childhood abuse memories should only be done with the help and guidance of a therapist.

Once you have remembered a childhood memory or memories and gained more understanding of yourself, it is time to take further steps to build your self-esteem, especially if you are stuck on dead center in weighing the decision to leave your celibate marriage.

THE SELF-ESTEEM SEESAW

Celibacy has probably taken its toll on your self-esteem. Your experience of being an unhappy celibate wife has undoubtedly diminished your concept of yourself as a woman, a wife, and a lover, and you need to marshal every possible method to build it back up.

Self-esteem is reflected in and influenced by everything you do. It is a part of every action and interaction, a barometer reflecting how you feel about yourself at any given time. Being complimented on the way you look or praised by your boss for a job well done feels great. On the other hand, when your husband tells you that he doesn't want to sleep with you, or he pushes your hands away, saying, "Don't touch me," your self-esteem as a woman is dashed to the ground.

All of your life experiences affect your self-esteem. Studies of successful women whose early years left much to be desired have shown that a positive experience—winning a scholarship, for example, or being commended and promoted on the job, or receiving a mentor's praise and trust—enhanced their self-esteem. To be recognized and appreciated by someone whose opinion you value moves your self-esteem a notch higher.

Think of your self-esteem as a work in progress. It is your challenge to pick up the tools—which are your strengths and talents—or to reach out for whatever help you need to rebuild your self-esteem. A strengthened sense of self-worth opens the door to making changes.

All of us have areas in our lives in which we feel competent and successful, whether at home, at work, at church, in a hobby, in sports, or in appearance. You may feel particularly confident about your ability to handle a crisis, or the way you decorate your home, or about your skills as an organizer or as a loving, nurturing person. With time, and many life experiences, you learn that you are more capable, worthy, and lovable than you imagined.

There are many ways for you to enhance your self-esteem, and there are many books on that subject. We offer several specific suggestions we have found helpful, and we hope as you read the material and complete the exercises, you will gain a more holistic view of your life and acquire the self-confidence to boost your decision-making ability.

The planning that goes into your decision to leave your celibate lifestyle should include the past, present, and future. We will help you to:

- identify your past successes and skills
- examine your fears and take risks, one at a time
- seek the support of a skilled therapist

Every Reason to Be Proud

You have many skills and abilities that you have used throughout your life. Recognizing them and claiming them with pride enhances your sense of worth. When we speak of skills or abilities, we do not mean technical skills such as operating a computer or becoming a musician or a dental hygienist. We mean the skills you use as you interact with other people and handle situations—for example, the way you organize your home or an event, or your ability to instruct or to listen caringly to someone. Perhaps such skills seem so natural to you that you do not recognize them as skills. Perhaps you discredit them and shrug off a compliment with "Oh, that was nothing." But that *is* something. Your skills are special and unique aspects of who you are. You need to recognize them as strengths you can build a career on, take credit for, and use as stepping-stones in building your self-esteem. Confidence in your skills can help you love yourself enough to get out of an unhappy and perhaps destructive celibate marriage.

The kinds of skills that we will help you identify and acknowledge with pride include:

negotiating	teaching	managing	persuading
arbitrating	selling	researching	organizing
initiating	nurturing	planning	implementing
listening	developing	coaching	problem solving

Joan shares an experience to help you get started. "When I was 16 I was asked to tell stories to young children at the library. I saw nothing unusual when the group of six children grew to 15, then 25, and finally 40 and we could no longer fit into the room at the library. I then arranged to use a nearby church hall, and soon that room was crowded with youngsters, many of whom were older than the original group. It was no longer feasible to entertain the various ages with the same material. I organized the children to perform for one another, doing skits, dances, and songs.

"I never gave my skills names, and neither did anyone else at the time. I had organized the group of children, directed them in their performances, initiated and negotiated a change of location, and supervised their activities. I was doing what came naturally to me at 16, and I didn't recognize these were inborn abilities I would use all of my life. Years later my therapist, whom I respected, pointed them out, commended me, and called me a 'creative organizer.' He then encouraged me to accept an interesting administrative position in which I could use my skills: organizing, supervising, initiating, problem solving, managing, and negotiating."

Using the exercise that follows, begin by identifying a particular achievement for which you felt proud and successful or received recognition and praise from others. Think about what specific skills you used to achieve this success. Naming them and then looking at how you use these same skills today will help you realize that you are a very capable woman with more talents and abilities at your disposal than you may have imagined.

Before you begin to work on this exercise, read the entire exercise through once or twice.

EXERCISE

The Path of Least Resistance

When you do something easily and when it is a pleasure to do, you are using your natural abilities. How often have you heard, "No pain, no gain"? The implication is that if a task is not difficult, if you haven't had to work hard to achieve something, it's of less or no value. We disagree. When you do what you love to do and what comes naturally, chances are you do it well and enjoy the doing. This exercise will illustrate how your skills surface and work for you. Once you can acknowledge how important they are, you can consider how to use them as you plan your future.

Skills are visible in everything you do, once you start looking for them. It might be easier to recall achievements if you divide your life into periods of time, such as before high school, between high school and marriage, and the time since your marriage. Single out situations in which you did something well and enjoyed doing it. Scan your life for such events. Use the list below to jog your memory.

1. A time when I was praised for a job well done
2. A time when people said I couldn't succeed but I did
3. A time when I felt proud
4. A time when I nurtured someone
5. A time when I felt afraid of doing something and did it anyway
6. A time when I solved a problem

7. A time when I reached out in friendship
8. A time when I made peace between people
9. A time when I knew the answer
10. A time when I felt recognized and valued

Select an event or achievement that made you feel good, useful, special, or successful. Write about it as if you were telling a story, with as much detail as you can recall. Write it from your personal viewpoint. Be sure to include all of your feelings. Savor the success of that moment. Your memory might begin like this:

When I was 14 I was in charge of organizing the Girl Scout picnic, and _____

_____

_____

Focus on the details of what you did in order to accomplish your task. Ask yourself: What was my achievement? What exactly did I do that made the situation successful? For example, did you sit down with two people who were not getting along and help them to resolve their differences? Did you come into a chaotic situation and take charge? Did you organize material that was confusing? Did you solve a problem for someone? You may recall having been praised for helping someone and you may say, "I only listened to them," not realizing that really listening to someone is a gift of love and appreciation and a significant skill for anyone in the helping professions. Recall any praise and recognition you may have gotten.

Make a list of the skills you have identified as your own. Can you see how you are using them in your life today, with other people and with situations that arise at work, at home, or in volunteering? List several skills in your journal and note how you have used them within the past year.

I used my skill of _____ when I _____ .

Can you see that your skills are very important parts of you, that you can draw on them to help further a career and in all aspects of your life?

Now make a list of the words that describe how you felt in recalling your skills. Did you feel proud, excited, capable, skillful, wise, creative, important, lovable? Use these positive feelings, and the skills you have identified, to write affirmations.

Affirmations are positive statements about yourself that you repeat often to help you build or reinforce your positive self-concept. Take three-by-five cards and write one affirmation on each card. They might read:

I now have the wisdom to make the right decision about my life.
I can create a good life for myself.
I make things happen, and I can get out of this marriage.
I nurture others and deserve to be nurtured as well.

Affirmation works, even if you're skeptical and feel foolish at first, because it is a way of thinking and acting "as if" what you are saying is already a fact. It is amazing how by repeating such statements you can change your self-image, become empowered, and feel in control of your life. Read these cards several times a day to remind yourself of how terrific and capable you are. Keep them where you can easily get to them—in your purse perhaps. Don't merely glance at them and rush through the words. Think about them, and when you do, throw back your shoulders, lift your head high, and see yourself as successful, imaginative, or nurturing. See it in your mind and you will come to believe it in your heart. This is one way you can begin to stretch in the cocoon of your celibate marriage, to break out of the darkness, and like a butterfly spread your wings and take flight—in this case, out of your unsatisfying, sexless marriage.

One Risk at a Time

Change is not easy to initiate. One way to get moving and to build self-esteem is by taking risks one small step at a time. This can be exciting as well as difficult, for it is frightening to take risks and to re-create your world. But you can reinvent your life, as Dr. David Viscott tells us in *Risking*, his book about making important choices. "Each person," he says, "must take the risk of creating a life of his own, assembling the best parts of the past and weaving them together into a story that has the most optimistic future."

Taking risks, one small risk at a time, is the next step in enhancing your self-esteem. Nothing builds self-confidence more than fearing something and doing it anyway. You will feel yourself grow, your self-esteem increasing with each fear you overcome. Fear limits your possibilities. It hangs over your life like a perpetual cloud. When you face up to a fear and challenge its power, you pierce a hole in the darkness. As you light up your life you take control and become stronger and more your own woman.

Perhaps some of your fears seem minor to you. After all, how important can it be to go to a movie alone? Some of your fears may be ones shared by many people: speaking up in a meeting, or flying, or asking for a raise. No matter how small or large the fear or how widely shared, as Susan Jeffers tell us in her book about courage, *Feel the Fear and Do It Anyway*, each time you master a fear you gain confidence in yourself. You are more secure about taking on one fear and then another, and your sense of competence grows.

The following exercise challenges you to reach beyond the limits of your daily routines.

EXERCISE ────────────────────────────────
Facing Fear Down and Out of Your Life

In your journal, make a list of things you are afraid to do. Your list should include fears you might dismiss as unimportant, like wanting to see a movie but feeling anxious and uncomfortable about going alone. Perhaps you avoid eating alone in a restaurant or driving on a four-lane highway. Maybe you are afraid to go river rafting or to exhibit your handicrafts in a local show. List any and all things you avoid doing out of fear. Make as long a list as you can think of, and go back and add to it as you remember more.

Now address each fear directly in your journal. Write about each fear in the manner illustrated below.

When I think about doing _____
I feel _____ because I am afraid that I will _____ .

Be totally honest with yourself in order to see exactly how much and why you are limiting yourself. Go a step further and ask yourself:

The worst thing that can happen to me if I do or go

_____ is _____.

As your next step, select one of your lesser fears and allow yourself a week to act on it. Tell yourself repeatedly, "I can do this." Leave a space in your journal so that after the event you can come back and write about what you did and how you felt.

I faced my fear of _____. _____ by
doing or going _____, and it felt _____ .

Before marrying Neal, Joan had enrolled in and then impetuously dropped out of a university in Maine. "Eight years later I was living in Maine again, my kids were in nursery school, and I decided to go back to college. I was terrified. The university had been the scene of what I considered a major failure. I decided to take it one class at a time and enrolled in Anthropology, a favorite subject. I arrived on campus the first day with clammy hands, my heart racing as it sank into the pit of my stomach. The crowded parking lot, the maze of buildings and classrooms, seemed unmanageable. As I forced myself out of my car I kept thinking, 'The worst thing that can happen to me is that I can't keep up with younger students and I might fail and drop out, again, but I'll survive.'

"But this didn't happen. I faced my fear of failure. I found the classroom, loved the academic atmosphere, loved the class, and got an A. I was jubilant. I felt as though I'd sprouted wings. From then on I went to college, wherever we lived, until I had my master's degree."

Each time you overcome a fear, take a risk, pursue a dream, no matter how small or large it seems to you, you empower yourself and increase your confidence in your ability to handle your life.

When Someone Listens

Another self-esteem–enhancing step is to talk to someone you like and trust, who will listen to you attentively, caringly, and not interrupt, criticize, or give you advice. You feel worthy when you feel heard. Having someone listen to you who believes in you and cares about you will make you feel that you are worth listening to, and your self-esteem quotient will rise. Verbalizing your feelings, and having those feelings reflected back to you by the listener, helps you face things you might be ignoring, or clarify things that are confusing, and this process moves you closer to making a reasoned decision about your life.

Diana asks, "Do you wonder what took me so long to get out of my marriage? In therapy, I discovered that I was bound by old mistaken ideas about what I could do and how things ought to be. My favorite childhood story was *The Little Engine That Could*. Like the little engine, I believed that I had the power to do anything I wanted to do as long as I worked hard enough and long enough. My efforts to fix our celibate marriage, although well-intentioned, had been in vain, for my husband was unwilling to look at his own behavior or make any substantial changes.

"Nowhere had I learned that I only had the power to change my *own* behavior or life. Realizing this was one of the most important steps I took toward being able to leave my marriage. I had felt powerless in my marriage, and this had caused me to doubt my ability to make a good life for myself.

"My therapist, an older, wiser woman, was comforting and helpful. She listened with such caring as I poured out my list of complaints about Ned's rages over any small thing; or the way he ridiculed my opinions, or mocked and scorned me in front of the children. We examined how, in spite of my successes at work or in the community, this verbal and emotional abuse took its toll and made me question my worth as a woman, a wage earner, and a mother.

"My therapist helped me identify my fears, some reasonable, some irrational, and make plans to overcome them. It was a blessing for me that I was working with a woman, for I feel that she understood life from a woman's perspective.

"She encouraged me to evaluate how celibacy had affected my life and how I felt about having a relationship with a man should I divorce. We realistically looked at the dangers of sex in this day of AIDS. I was overwhelmed by the shocking statistics, released by the Centers for Disease Control in March of 1992, reporting that one out of every eight hundred women and one of every one hundred men in America have already contracted HIV, the AIDS virus, and every 13 minutes someone else becomes infected."

The statistics shocked Diana into rethinking her options for sex in the future. She faced the possibility that with the AIDS epidemic in our country she might never want to risk having sex again.

TAKING ACTION—FROM MARRIED TO SINGLE

The time will come, maybe after months or years, when you have considered all the options, you have a clear picture of the role you want sex to play in your life, and you feel self-confident about your ability to stand alone. By taking the time to prepare for life as a single woman (perhaps a single mother), you have begun to face and overcome your fears and feel more confident about your ability to take control of your life. You are prepared to take action and are finally ready to hire a lawyer and leave your marriage.

Joan had worked for months with her therapist preparing to leave. "Once we rated the importance of sex as a seven, and acknowledged that the solution of having affairs had proven to be transitory and emotionally unsatisfying, my therapist focused our work on my achievements. We looked at my successes, like my tenacity in completing my education, and he helped me take credit for how well I had organized my home, my life, and any volunteer commitment I had ever made. My self-esteem grew, and I finally reached a stage where I could honestly say to myself or to anyone, 'I would rather live alone for the rest of my life than stay in this marriage.'

"Still, it was a gut-wrenching experience. My children had looked at me, their eyes a mixture of pain and anger. But I had been living an unhappy life in limbo and had reached a point of no return. Deciding to leave had been a freeing experience. Months later, when I walked out of the court a divorced woman, I felt as though I had climbed Mount Everest. My horizons seemed unlimited."

Tips for the Trip

As you read through this chapter, you may have reached the point where you feel more confident about your skills and your ability to plan a full life for yourself. You have learned to acknowledge your fears and act on them, and you may have decided that you can and should leave your celibate marriage. As you start your trip down the road to being single again, we would like to make a few suggestions.

1. *Cancel all regrets*. If you have been wistfully regretting lost years and time, stop doing that. Regret wastes energy. Acknowledge that you did what you could do when you were able to do it, and you could not have done it a moment sooner. You could not take the steps needed to bring about divorce until you had taken care of your grief work, learned to love yourself, and developed a greater sense of self-worth.

2. *Become financially savvy*. Don't take any precipitous action that might jeopardize your financial stability or your chil-

dren's futures. Approach divorce carefully and with serious consideration. A good attorney will ask you to gather information about your financial resources (how much money you will need to live on, how much you can reasonably expect to get from your husband, how much you can expect to earn yourself). Don't say, "I just want to get out of this marriage, I won't ask for much in the settlement." Know what you will need and let the attorney fight for what you deserve.

3. *Do it when it's best*. Time your move to divorce only when it is to your best advantage. You need to have an answer to these questions: How will I support myself? Do I need to retrain, complete my education, brush up on old, unused skills, or get a job? Have I carefully mapped out plans including where to live, how to manage with the children, how to obtain health insurance, and how to set up a realistic budget?

4. *Preserve familiar things*. If you are in the process of transition from being married to being single, take care of yourself in every way you can. When events are changing all around you, it is important to preserve familiar things. Sometimes that can be as simple as watching reruns of a favorite sitcom. Find and hang onto the little continuities that give structure to your days and nights: hot chocolate at bedtime, a regular hair appointment, Saturday movies with your kids, or that weekly phone call to your closest friend.

5. *Pamper yourself*. Be especially patient and kind to yourself. Treat yourself to things that are pleasurable—a weekend at a spa, a massage, a hot bath. Seek out people who lift your spirits. Work out at a gym or go hiking. Get tickets for a concert or play or go to an upbeat or funny movie. There are many pleasures in life. Reach out for yours and enjoy them.

6. *Love yourself first*. Chances are you have decided to divorce after years of unhappiness with many aspects of your

marriage. Once divorced, many women make up for lost time and rush out to find new sex partners. Don't do this. Remember the shocking statistics. Today one out of every one hundred men can infect you with the HIV virus, which can lead to full-blown AIDS. Today sex may cost you your life. Ask a new partner to have an AIDS test, and reciprocate by being tested yourself. Don't be swept away by passion and rush into sex: protect yourself with condoms and the spermicide, nonoxynol-9, available without a prescription. For complete, up-to-date information about all aspects of AIDS, call the Centers for Disease Control National Clearing House on AIDS at 1-800-458-5231.

Having given considerable thought and effort to making your decision, you may feel that leaving your celibate marriage is the best course of action or you may already have taken steps in this direction. On the other hand, you may still be uncertain that leaving is the best thing for you to do. Perhaps you wonder if it would be wiser to remain in your celibate marriage. You might be surprised to hear that many celibate wives have chosen to do just that.

There are many reasons why women decide to stay in marriages without sex. In the following pages you will meet such women as they build happy lives for themselves. But we are getting ahead of ourselves. Let them tell you in their own words!

Chapter 7

DECIDING TO STAY

* VICTORIA
Sex or no sex, I was not going to give up the financial security and the assets we both worked to accumulate over the years.

* LEE
It took me years to accept that I had an alcoholic husband and even longer to accept the fact that I could neither change nor control his behavior.

* ALICIA
I lived in unloving foster homes, so a stable home for my children has always come first. I grieved for the loss of sex, and it was a great accomplishment when I detached from Paul with grace and love.

* ELIZABETH
He was so sick, I felt duty bound to stay in my celibate marriage. I reached out to help myself with dancing lessons, which lifted my spirits, and my deep trust in God got me through the long years nursing him.

You may have worked through the exercises in chapter five and determined that you could resexualize your marriage, or you may have concluded that leaving your marriage is best for you. A third possibility is that you may have decided, for any number of reasons, to remain in your celibate marriage. If so, you are not alone. Many of the women we interviewed found happiness by accepting their celibacy and focusing their energies on other aspects of their lives: work, family, community or other creative endeavors. Under the right conditions, staying is as valid a choice as leaving. You have nothing to be ashamed about, for you are much more than your sexuality and no less a woman because you are not having sex in your marriage.

Friends and family may regard your decision as inaction or laziness. However, staying can be not a lack of decision, but a positive choice in favor of a viable marriage. Leaving implies that you have taken action to change your life, but in reality staying and feeling content with the decision requires an equally real internal change. While women who leave need to gain the courage and develop the resources to live alone, women who stay need the courage to accept their celibacy and emotionally detach while continuing to live with their husbands.

In the process of deciding to stay, you must also face and overcome any deep-seated prejudices against celibacy. We found that women who are at peace with their decision to stay married are not necessarily weak or dependent, or lacking in self-esteem and self-respect. They are capable women, most of whom are deeply involved in work, hobbies, or community activities.

The reasons women stay in celibate marriages include fear of being alone, financial support, health concerns, as well as social, family, and religious considerations. Some women stay because the marriage is loving or companionable; for others sex has become irrelevant. Any of these are valid reasons for staying if you can do so happily and with a sense of peace and contentment.

SOME WAYS OF BEING CELIBATE

We strongly believe that no one can tell a woman whether to stay in or leave her marriage without diminishing her personal power. Each woman must accept responsibility for her own life, and she chooses as she can, when she can, and not a moment sooner. In the following section, we will look at the lives of women offering their particular perspectives on staying married and being celibate. You may identify with how some women handle their lives under the following conditions:

A woman who stays in a highly dysfunctional marriage.
A woman who decides to stay temporarily.
A woman who explains her midlife view of celibacy.
A woman who enjoys a marriage of companionship without sex.

A Highly Dysfunctional Marriage

Most of the women we talked with who stay in celibate marriages are content with the status quo and have gone on to make fulfilling lives for themselves. But there are some who choose to stay and never come to any kind of satisfactory resolution. They remain angry or frustrated and wage perpetual battles on several fronts with their spouses.

John Bradshaw, host of the nationally televised PBS series

"Bradshaw on the Family" and author of the national bestsellers *On the Family* and *Homecoming,* considers all families to be dysfunctional to a lesser or greater degree.

Initially, *dysfunctional* was a word used to describe families characterized by alcoholism or drug use. Today the term has been popularized and extended to include all kinds and degrees of dis-ease in family relationships: physical or verbal abuse, continuing battles over finances, control, family, children, or sex issues; communication failures and absent fathers; and divorce.

Many people would consider a celibate marriage dysfunctional, and we agree with them when the marriage is filled with strife and volatile confrontation. This was the case in the marriage of Rachel and Cal, both materialistic, ambitious, successful professionals in their forties.

Rachel and Cal brought to their relationship the same degree of combative behavior they applied in the courtroom as trial attorneys. From the earliest days of their marriage they maintained an irascible attitude toward each other, fighting for control, arguing about where to live, where to vacation, how to raise the children, how to allocate their finances, and even where to be buried. Four years into the marriage they had two children and had hired a live-in housekeeper. Both spouses were competitively pursuing their law careers.

From the beginning, sex was part and parcel of their discord. Cal was prudish, his sexual behavior limited to a few kisses and intercourse. "Sex was over before I started," Rachel told us. "Cal would then rush into the shower as if he were contaminated by our contact. I felt resentful and frustrated, but for years I went on arguing and insisting that he should feel differently about sex and his body, and I persisted in believing that I could bring him around to seeing sex differently."

Rachel and Cal continued in this unsatisfactory pattern for

years. As Rachel's life got busier, she thought less about sex. She described the final episode of their sex life. "We had each won difficult cases in court and celebrated with an elegant dinner at the most expensive restaurant in town. I felt sexy, and I let Cal know this. When we got home he said he would run to the drugstore for condoms (the only form of contraception he would use). Three hours later when he finally returned, I was enraged. 'I thought you knew I was going to stop at the office,' he offered as explanation. 'Go to hell,' was all I could manage, and I decided right then that I would never again lower myself to ask for sex. That was six years ago."

We asked Rachel why they stayed married. "Why not stay? I respect Cal's brilliant mind. It's a challenge to debate with him. Our lifestyle is elegant, we have all the good things we want, money, prestige, intelligent children. I'm a divorce attorney and I've seen what divorce does to children and I don't want that for my kids." She reflected, "I doubt if we could live with someone else. My mother says we deserve each other."

Relationships emotionally bankrupted by conflict and rage are destructive to the partners and their children. We don't believe couples should stay together when they cannot resolve their differences and cannot live together without seriously damaging each other, physically or emotionally. If you are a woman caught up in the type of perpetual warfare Rachel and Cal so perfectly illustrate, we strongly urge you to seek professional help to identify the devastating games you and your husband are playing and to learn why you continue to put yourselves and your children through such an emotional meat grinder.

Deciding to Stay Temporarily

You may be one of those celibate wives who decide to stay in your celibate marriage while you prepare for divorce. You may need to complete your education in order to get a job or upgrade your skills to get a better-paying job. You may feel you need time to carefully plan how and where you will live and to save enough money to get started on your own. You may want to wait until your youngest child has finished high school.

If you choose to stay temporarily, chances are you are a younger celibate wife—in your twenties, thirties, or forties. You believe that there is a wide range of options open to you and that it will take time to sort through these options carefully as you plan for your future.

Whether you stay another two years or five years, if you don't learn to live in peace with yourself and your celibacy, the continuing stress will take its toll on your physical and/or emotional health. The ulcers, headaches, high blood pressure, heart disease, or depression that can result may block your efforts to leave no matter how well you've planned for divorce. Resolve now to make internal peace one of your priorities and work carefully through the exercises in this chapter. Later in the chapter we will show you how to stop controlling your husband, how to detach from emotions that make you miserable, and how to take responsibility for your own future.

Rickie is a 30-year-old celibate wife who would face serious financial difficulties if she left her marriage today, so she has decided to defer divorce and tolerate her marriage until she has completed her education.

Rickie is determined to get out of her five-year marriage after discovering her husband, Sam, in their bed with another woman a year ago. He had told her sarcastically that he liked variety and she'd better get used to it. Taking the AIDS epidemic seriously, Rickie had herself tested (results were negative), and then refused to sleep with Sam again. She began to make careful plans for leaving and raising her daughter as a single parent.

"Sam told me he would go to jail before he'd pay me a penny in support. I believe him. I work as a manicurist part time to pay for going to college at night. It may take me three more years until I get my degree in business. My daughter will be in elementary school, and then I'm out of here."

A Midlife View of Celibacy

At 50 or 60, a woman's perspective is very different from that of a woman in her 30s or 40s. Many feel that their options have narrowed. Is it logical to assume that she can find another man who will be sexually competent and meet her other needs as well? What are her career options? Can she expect to earn a decent wage? Can she count on her health being vigorous enough to sustain her through long periods of stress while going through a divorce and starting life over again? Does she really want to choose a financially reduced lifestyle, just when she and her husband are beginning to reap the financial rewards of 25 or 30 years of hard work? Victoria put it bluntly. "After all these years, when things are much better, even without sex, I will not give up my financial security and end up living in some crummy apartment, struggling to make ends meet."

Victoria had moved from her parents' to her husband's home when she was an overly dependent 18-year-old. For many years she deferred to Roger, her salesman husband, for everything. She put her life and decision-making on hold whenever he was out of town.

The passion and vigor of their early sexuality diminished over the years as Roger would return from sales trips tired and almost passionless. Victoria eagerly shared her story with us. "Those were tough years. I was alone with the kids and harried, and I lived for Roger to come home. Then I dumped all my problems on him, expected him to want to make love every night, and when he didn't I accused him of infidelity and was furious with him. After a while he came home to an armed truce, and to appease me went through the motions of making love when I insisted on it. I got tired of always asking, and we stopped having sex about five years ago."

When one of their sons was severely injured in an accident, Roger was not there through the anxious, lonely periods at the hospital; he wasn't there as Victoria handled lawyers, doctors, and insurance companies. She was 36 then and her self-confidence had grown. "That's when I grew up and knew I could stand on my own two feet."

Victoria began to reach out in her community. She joined Toastmasters public-speaking group to help overcome her shyness; she researched her Rumanian background, joined an ethnic club and learned the songs and foods of her ancestors. She turned her talents at the sewing machine into making one-of-a-kind party dresses for little girls, which earned her a small income and satisfying friendships with mothers and daughters as she continued making their special dresses from first-grade recitals through senior proms.

There had been years when Victoria and Roger hardly communicated. Victoria had considered divorce, then decided that her options had dwindled with age. Her future offered her a view of a possibly lonely, aging woman struggling to make ends meet, and this frightening image overshadowed all other frustrations and disappointments in her marriage, including sex.

As Victoria's life broadened, with new interests and people, her dependency diminished, as did her need for her husband's attention and for sex. Her relationship with Roger mellowed and became more companionable. Victoria felt a new sense of contentment within her marriage as well as in other areas of her life.

"I've reached a stage," she said, "where I am very sympathetic toward my gray-haired, tired husband who is still traveling, and even without sex, I have come to terms with our relationship and have let go the anger I used to vent on him. We now share a companionship unattainable in those early, difficult years."

Letting Go with Love

Some people believe that with no sex there is no marriage. We disagree. A viable marriage is much more than sexual intercourse. Into the tapestry of a marriage many threads can be woven: companionship, joy in family activities, and satisfying work (paid or volunteer). The result is a happy life. Having the option of finding happiness within a celibate marriage is important, for each woman's situation is unique, and only she can best evaluate and decide how to live her life.

Beth, 54, described her 21-year marriage to Joel. "I was miserable for years and forever raging with anger at Joel. I bitched and complained and was nasty to him. Joel wasn't open, warm, or affectionate enough; I had to drag an 'I love you' out of him. I felt he lacked drive and ambition, and it enraged me when he let people take advantage of him. He was stubborn, and an investment he made against my wishes cost us a lot of money. I felt betrayed when I had differences with other people and he never took my side. We were very different; I was emotional, he was impassive, yet during all those angry years we were having good sex."

Beth became so miserable trying to change Joel that she decided she either had to divorce him or find peace in her marriage. Over the years Beth had seen several therapists and had resisted changing her attitude. In her view, the problem was Joel's and *he* should change.

Information about codependency, popularized in the media in the past few years, offered her a new view of marital conflict and lit a spark that proved an eye-opener. Beth recognized herself as codependent, both controlling and caretaking, feeling responsible for Joel and everything else in their lives. "I blamed Joel for my unhappiness and I felt angry, victimized, and unappreciated."

Beth was appalled when she identified herself as a controlling, obsessive person, and the words of her therapists began to make sense. One day it all came together: Beth finally understood that if she wanted to find peace in her marriage she had to assume responsibility for herself and give up trying to control Joel. She stopped badgering or cajoling him to do what she wanted, and she stopped demanding his time and attention.

Controlling was a part of her, like her right arm, and in learning to accept and relinquish control, she grieved its passing and emerged from the process detached but with love. "It was total liberation. My feelings toward Joel changed. I stopped being angry and complaining. Our relationship changed completely. When we stopped fighting, we relaxed and began to talk to each other. Our marriage became infused with a spirit of good will and cooperation, and sex became more enjoyable."

Then four years ago Beth had vaginal surgery and sex became uncomfortable. "At first I didn't say anything. I thought it would get better with time. It didn't, and when I finally told Joel, he began to worry about hurting me." Beth lost interest in sex. Joel was willing and able, but could take it or leave it.

Beth told us that she and Joel were getting along well, and even without sex their life was a happy one. She had seen a doctor recently who explained that sometimes surgery changed the depth and shape of the vagina. He recommended trying different positions, and Beth and Joel plan to experiment to find a way in which Beth can enjoy sex without discomfort. Even if they never have sex again, Beth assured us, their marriage is a good one. They are committed to each other and happy to stay together.

THREE GIANT STEPS TO SERENITY

As you read Victoria's and Beth's stories, you may wonder what the secret is to finding peace and contentment within a celibate marriage. There are three important skills to master on the road to contentment. You must:

1. break free of your need to control anyone but yourself, especially your husband;
2. detach or emotionally disengage—from your husband, your sexuality, or anything that stands in the way of your serenity; and
3. assume responsibility for your own life by taking risks and making changes.

In the rest of this chapter we will explore these issues of control, detachment, and personal responsibility.

Control in the Name of Love

In the name of love and with the best of intentions, women frequently assume the responsibility for what happens within their marriages and families. They try to control others—because they need to make life happen as they want it to, or because they are trying to be helpful, or because they are sure they know what is right for everyone in the family. Some women control from positions of power, dominating their families, making or influencing all important decisions, certain that they know best. Other women control by guilt, making their husbands and children feel guilty for what they have done or haven't done. Others manipulate their families by appearing weak and helpless but being covertly in control.

Control is a double-edged sword. When you think you are controlling your husband, he is controlling you by his behavior without even trying. For example, let's assume your husband drinks. You count the number of drinks he's had. You try to keep him from buying more alcohol. You worry about how much he'll drink at the party on Saturday night. You push him to go to AA. He does as he pleases, while you waste tense and exhausting hours obsessing over the problem.

Perhaps your husband is not attentive or affectionate and hides behind the newspaper every evening. You nag and agitate to get his attention, to no avail. In silence and anger, you overeat. He ignores the situation, and you end up overweight and still unhappy. Your time, energy, and efforts are wasted: you don't get his attention but he certainly gets a lot of yours.

Giving up control is a hard concept to grasp and even harder to put into practice. You are sure if you let go of the reins of control in certain areas of your life, things will get worse and fall apart—and they might. But consider the heavy burden of having to be in control. Your attention is focused on others and not yourself. You are living their lives, not your own. You feel like a martyr and a victim, unappreciated and often misunderstood. Conversely, giving up control of events and people allows you to claim your own life and invest your energy in self-fulfilling things.

Lee is an illustration of the "perfect" wife, always making things right, trying to keep everything and everyone under control, who finally learned how futile this was. Lee talked about her 33-year marriage to Harvey, an alcoholic politician. "We had our kids and material things, which compensated for other problems in the relationship. Sex was available only when Harvey wanted it, much less often than I would have liked. By the time we were married 15 years, sex was about once every three months. Harvey insisted we sleep in separate beds, and the lack of sex was a constant source of arguments." Lee and Harvey have been celibate for six years.

Lee became consumed with Harvey's problems. She worried that others would notice his drinking. She assumed the thankless job of remembering things for him, making excuses for him, doing his dirty work when he had to fire an employee, buffering his relations with the children, making excuses when he needed an out in a social situation.

Because Harvey had seemed to be a social drinker, it was many years before Lee recognized that he was an alcoholic. It was another year before she started attending an Al-Anon program, where she learned to stop taking responsibility for Harvey's behavior.

It took months of Al-Anon meetings and seeing a private therapist before Lee was ready to admit that she could not control Harvey or anyone but herself. She decided to stop rescuing Harvey, to say no when she meant no, and to allow him to learn from his own mistakes. Lee realized that in trying to control Harvey she was so focused on his problems that she had abandoned her interests and had no life of her own. After much resistance, Lee accepted the fact that she could not control anything but her own thoughts and behaviors—not the way things turned out, not life itself, and certainly not the behavior of another person.

With each letting go Lee gained strength and courage. When she stopped picking up the pieces for Harvey, the world didn't fall apart. Her energy, which had been wasted overseeing her husband's behavior, was freed up. She invested in herself. Lee began to set goals for herself, deal with her feelings, and process her disappointments and grief. She identified exactly what activities brought her pleasure and satisfaction and concentrated her time and energy on these.

Lee rebounded from her role as martyr in her dysfunctional marriage with an irrepressible zest for life. Encouraged by family and friends, she opened first one, then two thriving day-care centers. She was exhilarated by her success and relished the freedom of being relieved of responsibility for controlling Harvey's and her children's lives. She loved her husband, but as she focused on taking control of her own life and happiness, she felt less and less interested in sex, and she was able to emotionally disengage from him.

At one point, when the children were grown, Lee separated from Harvey. She supported herself as they lived apart for almost a year. She enjoyed the freedom, going and coming as she pleased, but something was missing. "I could support myself, I could live alone, but I missed the sense of belonging a family brings, and I missed Harvey and our life together."

Harvey had joined AA and was now sober, but nothing had changed sexually and Lee still faced celibacy in their marriage. She asked herself, "What is the worst thing that can happen to me if I never have sex again?" Her answer was, "Why, my life is filled with so many things, I'll do just fine." Lee concluded that other things mattered more than sex: financial security, the social status of being a politician's wife, grandparenting as a couple, her religious convictions that said marriage was for better or worse, and her basic affection for Harvey.

As Lee learned, there are ways to help yourself as you take steps toward giving up control. In freeing others to be who they are, you can set yourself free to be the best possible person you can be. Begin by following these suggestions:

1. *Control your thoughts.* Stop obsessing about what your husband does or does not do. Make yourself, not him, the center of your thoughts. You do have the power to take charge of your mind and control what you are thinking. Stop fixating on things he has (or has not) done or said, and deliberately force yourself to think about something that is pleasurable to you. Say to yourself over and over, "I cannot make him do what I want. He is the product of his own upbringing. I release him and let him go."

2. *Break the cycle.* When you see yourself beginning to react and argue about the same old issues, stop talking and remove yourself physically from the scene. However, do not sit and stew in another room. Do something that gives you pleasure: take a walk, call a friend, or turn to a hobby. Go into your room, put on music you enjoy and then move or dance to it. This is a great way to release tension and divert your mind.

3. *Change your expectations.* Stop expecting your husband to act as you would like him to. Stop hoping he will express feelings he never has expressed before. Allow him to be himself. Ask yourself, How many hours have I wasted trying to change him? Has it worked? If you spend another 10 years trying to change your husband it will make no difference, for each of us nurses and cherishes our own particular beliefs.

4. *Make affirmations.* Make affirmation cards that assert, "I let go my need to control my husband, and I am serene," and "I accept my husband for who he is and I am at peace." Add other cards that apply to your own situation. Read your cards several times a day. At first this may seem an artificial practice; you may say, "But that's not how I feel." It is the way you need to feel if you are to break the bonds of control that tie you to unhappiness in your marriage.

180

We realize these changes in your behavior will take a while to achieve, but they are worth your time and effort. We cannot emphasize strongly enough the fact that no matter how hard you try, you cannot effect a permanent change in another person.

Perhaps you are not aware of how much or in what ways you persist in your controlling behavior. The following exercise will help you to see how you try to control your husband's behavior, how you feel about doing so, and how effective your attempts at control are.

EXERCISE
Setting Yourself Free

Look back over the past month and identify incidents in which you felt you had to control your husband's behavior. Did they have to do with how he spends money, his drinking or taking drugs, his work, or his relationship with you or the children? These are some common areas in which many women try to exert control, but you may have other areas in which you feel responsible for the outcome of events.

Select one or two incidents and title them, as if you were going to write a story about each one. Write the title across the top of a page in your journal. Remembering a time when Harvey drank, Lee wrote, "Making Harvey Go to Mildred's Dinner." Answer the following questions about each incident:

Did it work?
Did it result in permanent change?
How do I feel having to be responsible for another adult's behavior?

181

Do I want to carry the burden of this responsibility for the rest
of my life? If not, why not?

What am I afraid will happen if I can't control my husband's
behavior?

Read over what you have written. Can you see how useless
your efforts were? Lee pressured Harvey into going to dinner at
Mildred's, then was humiliated when he drank heavily, dozed
off, and snored in front of the hostess.

In doing this exercise you will see exactly the control games
you and your husband play. Once you recognize them you can
begin to break the cycle. When you see a similar situation
starting to happen, consciously change your behavior. You can
do this by changing the subject or leaving the room, as you
remind yourself that you do not have the power to change your
husband. You may feel better if you spend a few minutes
ventilating your feelings by writing in your journal. Remind
yourself how useless and frustrating all your efforts have been to
impose your will on your husband. He is as sure his way is right
as you are sure yours is right. Let it be. Give up and gain peace.

Detaching but Continuing to Care

If you are agonizing about your celibacy or your seemingly
unsolvable, unhappy relationship—if you feel pressed to the wall
or hanging by a thread, yet you want to stay in your marriage—
detachment should be your goal. We have found that women
who live contentedly in celibate marriages have emotionally
detached from their husbands and from their own sexuality.

Detachment, in the sense we are using it, means to let go,
to emotionally remove yourself from a situation. Marriage and
family therapist Manfred Mueller of Durham, North Carolina,

assures his clients that "No one should adjust, make do, or settle for celibacy unless they can do so with detachment and love." He feels couples can attain this detachment through a thoughtful examination of their beliefs and feelings, which leads to a full acceptance of the partner, and Mueller guides his clients toward this goal.

To achieve such acceptance, you will have to take a hard look at your life and recognize the things that you cannot change. In the preceding exercise you learned that you cannot control another person, including your spouse. Accepting this truth about your husband and your marriage is a major step on the path to detachment. Unfortunately, when a woman is presented with the concept of detachment, she often feels confused and resistant. She thinks, If I do that I just won't care, so what's the point of staying at all?

But look at the kinds of changes that can take place, however slowly, with detachment, changes that come from deep within yourself:

1. You can forgive and develop empathy for your husband's flaws and insecurities. For example, you may realize that his emotional distance stems from the fact that his mother abandoned the family when he was four, and he distrusts closeness for fear of further abandonment.
2. You can reorganize your life and focus on what is right with you rather than what is wrong with him. This enhances your sense of personal power. You can fill your life with those people and things that bring you happiness. You can say, "I am responsible for creating my own happiness and living my own life. I will be happy."

Acceptance of your husband is an act of will, while detachment is a feeling that comes after you have accepted him and given up trying to change him. When you have adequately grieved over the loss of sex in your marriage and accepted your husband for the person he is, you can then arrive at that state called detachment. One day, perhaps suddenly but most often after a period of time, perhaps with the help of a therapist, something happens: you realize that you have detached. A change has taken place within yourself. You see your life as if through new eyes. It's like being at the theater when the curtain goes up on the second act. The play and the characters are the same, but the set and the mood are different. When you detach you become a different, happier woman. The ache is gone. You don't feel enraged or desperate any longer. You no longer care if your husband does what you want him to do. You recognize and accept the fact that he is a product of his own early years and family upbringing and you cannot change the way he thinks or acts. Things that upset you before now elicit little or no response. You no longer feel like a victim or a martyr, for you are no longer blown about by the winds of his behavior. You no longer react to your husband in negative, painful ways that deprive you of joy or plunge you into despair. That is fundamental self-care. That is detachment.

You may ask a very important question: If I detach will I still care? It isn't easy to find the balance, to remove yourself emotionally from your husband while continuing to care for him. You want to find a resolution; you want to stay married but without the anger and agitation that characterize your relationship. Even as you give up the painful emotions associated with trying to change things between you and your husband, you want to hold on to all the good things in your marriage. When you detach you move away emotionally but with a sense of peace rather than hostility. Your husband isn't your lover anymore, but he may still be your friend.

Detachment, when it happens, comes from a place deep within. It is accompanied by a sense of relief, a burden lifted, worry ceased. It is suddenly okay not to need to control or influence your husband, and you no longer say things like, "He's self-centered and selfish," or "He'd be okay, if only he would . . ." All the things that irritated and angered you, made you unhappy, provoked arguments, and caused stress in your marriage now brush lightly across the surface of your emotions, without impact. You are living your own life, in the moment, now, and though the focus is on yourself you can still retain affection and concern for your husband.

Melody Beattie, discussing detachment in *Codependent No More,* tells us what detachment is *not.* "Detachment," she says, "is not cold, hostile withdrawal; a resigned, despairing acceptance of anything life and people throw our way. . . . Detaching does not mean we don't care. It means we learn to love, care and be involved without going crazy. . . . We become free to care and to love in ways that help others and don't hurt ourselves."

The most peaceful, well-adjusted, and, yes, the happiest celibate wives we know are those who accept their husbands as they are and feel detached from the overall problem of sexuality. They no longer fight with their husbands about sex. If at times they still feel cheated or deprived of sex, they no longer allow the lack of sex to control or diminish their lives. Some women handle their sexual desires by masturbating, some have an active fantasy life, some try to meet their needs outside of their marriages, others have simply lost all interest in sex. Alicia, celibate for 18 of her 38 years of marriage, claims a hard-won detachment from her indifferent husband and her sexuality. Alicia has refocused her hopes and dreams on other aspects of her life, like family and community involvement.

Orphaned at five, the victim of sometimes abusive foster

185

homes, Alicia's commitment to provide her four children with a stable, nurturing home and family superseded sex in her life. Extroverted, exuberant, and affectionate, Alicia's personality is in direct contrast to that of her physician husband, Paul, who is restrained, controlled, and pragmatic.

From the beginning, Paul, though kind, was undemonstrative; he made it clear that his interest in sex was perfunctory and having children was its goal. "Early in the marriage Paul and I fought a lot," Alicia recalled. "Sex was not satisfying or often enough. I felt no sense of intimacy or love, yet I deluded myself that I had enough love and passion for both of us and I could change him. It took me years to realize that Paul was not rejecting me as a woman, he was uninterested in sex, and we drifted into a pattern of sex every few months."

Paul proved to be a caring and concerned father, and as Alicia stopped questioning what she was doing wrong, she began to reconcile herself to their lengthening periods of celibacy. Her commitment to her children strengthened. Always an optimist, Alicia stopped nagging Paul, maintained a cheerful home, and counted her blessings. "I felt blessed to have a home of my own, a reliable if unexpressive husband, and especially when they were little, the loving arms of babies seemed like heaven."

Alicia explained, "I kept hoping my open expressions of love for Paul would elicit the same from him. I used to try to set up situations that would force expressions of affection from him. Then I gave that up and I looked at his family background and asked myself, 'How would I feel if I had parents who never touched, who hardly spoke to each other or their children, who punished severely and permitted no dancing or singing in their children's lives?' I began to get a whole new perspective about

Paul and to realize that unless he went for therapy, he would never change."

Alicia wondered at their uniqueness, the way each of them had been influenced by their childhoods—she, deprived of love, yet needing and wanting to nurture others and express affection and love; Paul, similarly deprived, withdrawn and unable to show his feelings.

By their tenth year of marriage, Alicia no longer felt totally frustrated, angry, and rejected. One day, sadly and in acceptance, she had said to Paul in her mind, "I won't demand affection or pressure you anymore." She still cared for him but she had come to terms with his inability to show his feelings. Alicia's need for intimacy and sex with Paul diminished and gradually became a thing of the past. Eighteen years ago she and Paul stopped having sex and moved into separate bedrooms.

Alicia had gone through a process familiar to many celibate wives. First she counted on Paul changing, then felt angry when he did not. She spent years fighting with him. Then she withdrew, suffered in silence, and hardened her heart. She knew she would never ask Paul for a divorce. Eventually she hit emotional rock bottom and realized that since leaving had never been an option, for her own peace of mind she must let go of both her need to change Paul and her sexuality.

"I grieved for my loss of sex and my dreams of a loving marriage, and I worked hard to accept my situation and to detach myself from Paul, to understand how his puritanical background contributed to who he is. For example, I stopped putting my arms around him, because when he stiffened and ignored me it hurt so much. I consider it a great accomplishment that I came to accept him with grace and love. In time I came to feel that even without sex, and all the other emotional involvement with a man, I could still reach out with love to others."

Alicia turned within, drawing on her deep faith, and turned outside as well, to friends and involvement in the community to fill her life with meaningful activity. She devoted herself to raising her children and threw her energy into helping people. Although not connected with a specific religious denomination, Alicia is a deeply spiritual woman who has become known for her kindness and generosity: visiting the sick and cooking and cleaning for them, sharing her food and clothing, opening her heart and home to homeless children. She appealed to Paul and his medical colleagues for free care for the needy people she took under her wing.

Alicia is no different from many women who feel cheated of intimacy and sex and consider affairs unacceptable. She learned to give her life meaning through other people and satisfying work. In summing up her life Alicia said, "My children and grandchildren have always been most important to me, and what helped me through the really tough and lonely years was my faith in God and a strong trust that my life had a deeper meaning."

As you read Alicia's story of hard-won serenity, you may wonder how far you have come on the road to detachment. This exercise will help you answer that question.

EXERCISE
How Detached Am I?

In your journal number a page from 1 to 8. Answer True for any of the statements that apply to you and your husband in the past several months.

1. We seem to have the same disagreements again and again.
2. My husband seems to know how to easily upset me and does so frequently.

3. I am very concerned about how other people view our marriage.
4. I feel as if I am riding an emotional roller-coaster, happy when my husband is out of the house, and upset when he is home.
5. My husband has several habits or behaviors that continue to annoy me.
6. I am very sensitive to my husband's moods and try not to upset him.
7. I love my husband and know that if I can only find the right information in a book or a good counselor, he'll understand how he hurts me and he'll change.
8. When my husband is happy, I feel happy too. When he is down or depressed, I feel my good mood slipping away.

Answering True to any of these statements is a sign that you still need to work at severing that emotional attachment that causes you unhappiness in your celibate marriage. When you have reached detachment the items above will no longer be true for you and your husband.

Love and Affection Without Sex

Most of the women we talked with who stayed in their celibate marriages had husbands who refused sex. But there are marriages in which it is the woman who would prefer not to have sex, or who prefers sex considerably less often than her husband but wants to remain in the marriage, as Marcy did.

Marcy and Jeff, a couple in their thirties, are an outstanding example of detachment with love. Married 14 years, they are a caring, devoted couple, compatible in every way but sexually. They have exerted every effort to work out sexual incompatibilities yet have become celibate, but they remain deeply involved

189

with each other and their three children. One of their children is a special-needs child, on whom much of their love and attention is focused.

Marcy is the partner whose sex drive is considerably lower. Marcy told us that she never enjoyed sex and always felt more of an observer than a participant. Individual therapy, she explained, helped her to identify the obstacles blocking her enjoyment of sex. "I could list all the problems: I was suffering from perform-ance anxiety, approval needs, insecurity about conveying my sexual needs to Jeff, and I was never able to live up to my desire to be the perfect sex partner."

Yet knowing all this changed nothing. When they tried sex therapy, Jeff resisted. He was never comfortable with what he considered the managed aspect of sexual therapy. Marcy recalled, "He felt he was being asked to perform mechanically."

"During many months of couples counseling," Marcy told us, "we came to terms with the fact that my sex drive was naturally lower than Jeff's and that was normal for me, just like wanting sex often was normal for Jeff. What to do about it was the problem, for we were and are committed to our children and to this marriage, and we've trusted each other and always been able to communicate."

Acceptance and detachment brought Marcy and Jeff sur-cease from sexual tension. In therapy Jeff determined he was tired of having his strong sex drive control him. He decided it was a case of mind over matter, and because he loved Marcy and did not want a divorce, he set to work to change his mind. Marcy was pleased to tell us, "We have forged strong bonds of love and commitment to each other, our marriage, and our children, so we've decided to remain together. Though there are times when I would be willing, I accept the fact that Jeff now finds it easier to be totally celibate. We stay busy. We both work and are heavily involved with our children and have thrown ourselves into community activities."

ACCEPTING PERSONAL RESPONSIBILITY

It takes courage to assume responsibility for your own decisions and your own life. Many of us, especially those in our mid- or later years, were conditioned by our upbringing to be satellites of a man. We become the earth to his sun. But within each of us there is power, and we can tap this source to light our own way.

Taking responsibility means being honest with yourself as you stop rationalizing, "My life's not so bad," or "I know other women who have it worse," or "Sex is not so important to me." You can say instead, "It is important to me, but there are other factors, in addition to celibacy, that are also important, and I am making a choice to stay in this marriage because . . ."

Being responsible for yourself can feel lonely. Making unilateral decisions that change your life and possibly the lives of your children can be frightening. Trying new things and making mistakes can be upsetting; you may not have been trained to expect mistakes as a necessary and important part of your learning experiences. But you can learn from your mistakes, and with each risk you take and each success you have, your courage increases, and you gain confidence in your ability to re-create your life for and by yourself, as Kay did.

Kay courageously approached us in a restaurant where we were eating and making plans for this book. She came over, apologized for intruding, and said she had overheard us and was curious about the book we were writing. When we explained, her face lit up and she declared herself to be a celibate wife of over 20 years. "Interview me," she said.

We ached, listening to Kay tell of the young bride so cruelly

191

rejected on her honeymoon. "Sex was very fast. I felt nothing at all, except that it hurt me. Hugh was furious at me and called me stupid. Later when I knew more and tried to approach him he screamed at me, 'Oh, so now you want it—you bitch. To hell with you.' After that I never enjoyed sex and lost all drive to have it."

Twenty years is a long time to live in a sexually barren marriage. Kay shared her feelings with us. "For years I hated my life, I hated sex. I hated him, and yet I felt sorry for him because he'd been physically and emotionally abused as a child." Kay gradually came to terms with her celibacy, and as she did she chose to shut out all sexual feelings, thoughts, talk, movies, and books. "I gave up on sex years ago. Celibacy is a very Catholic idea, and I'm like a nun with a bonus—my children and grand-children, who are a blessing to me."

When her children were teenagers Kay started therapy. It was only then that she came to understand that her low self-esteem and dependency that trapped her in her dysfunctional marriage were rooted in childhood verbal abuse from her mother. Kay told us, "My mother had hammered at me, 'No one likes you; you're too bony—who would ever want you? You talk too much; you don't know anything.'" Kay had accepted these diatribes as truth and had carried this picture of herself into her marriage, where she exchanged her mother for Hugh and accepted his verbal abuse as no worse than what she deserved.

There were years of unhappiness and thoughts about leaving, and even one abortive attempt, when Kay tried to rent an apartment but retreated in panic when she figured that she'd never make it financially as a single parent. "In therapy I came to terms with my own low self-esteem, but even when I was successful and felt good about myself, leaving was no longer an option," she said. "I realized that initially I had stayed with Hugh out of fear that I couldn't make it with the children alone. I felt guilty about separating the children from their father, and as a Catholic, I felt obliged to make the best of it. Later, when I understood how my difficult childhood had affected me, I could forgive him and feel compassion for him because I knew the terrible life he'd had. Since, by then, I had no interest in sex, I saw no reason to give up the marriage. Hugh had mellowed, possibly due to medication, and our relationship was calm though distant. My goals, which I had achieved, had been, 'I will stop reacting to Hugh, I will remain indifferent to sex, and I will make a good life for myself.' "

To do this, Kay changed her behavior. She disengaged; she refused to be the target any longer. She listened to Hugh's words and reminded herself that they derived not from anything she had done, but from his own festering discontent. Kay proudly told us, "It was a red-letter day when I realized I had detached from Hugh. He yelled at me for some minor incident and I felt nothing. My stomach didn't harden into a knot. I didn't feel angry and want to strike back, I just felt aloof and indifferent to what was going on, free and lighthearted."

If we, as therapists, had counseled Kay when she was 25 or 30 and miserable, we would have encouraged her to get out of her marriage. But how could we give such counsel to a 60-year-old who had made difficult choices and built a good life around those choices, and who feels satisfied with her achievements and lifestyle today?

The longer we knew Kay, the more apparent it became that she had made a good life for herself. As she had worked at assuming more and more responsibility for her own life and happiness, she had begun to do things she liked: making new friends, traveling alone or on art tours, taking watercolor lessons, going back to college and eventually earning a master's in fine arts. It was as if she had drawn a map clearly outlining the path to her future happiness. Kay's energies poured into creative work, and today she is a successful watercolorist and proud owner of an art gallery. Kay told us, "An astonishing thing happened. I realized I was happy. My life had become increasingly interesting. I was still living with Hugh; I was still celibate but I didn't care."

Should Kay have left her marriage? Perhaps. But she did not choose to do so, even after she had therapy, and we respect her decision, though at first when we talked with her we were appalled at her story of verbal abuse. But Kay brimmed with optimism and was without self-pity, and it became clear that she had created a full and satisfying life for herself.

Can you accomplish such a major change in attitude and behavior if you decide to stay in your celibate marriage? Of course you can—many women have. You will need to develop new goals and take steps to implement them.

For a few days, listen to how many times you say, "I wish " or "I want" or "I hope," and contrast this with the number of times you say, "I will." The only truly effective, life-changing statement is "I will." "I will" is the starting point for change. "I will start my own savings account. I will get some help for myself. I will upgrade my skills and get a better-paying job."

"I will" is a clear statement of how you will get there, but you need to know exactly where you want to go and what you want to do. You need a map or blueprint around which you can begin to organize and chart a course for your life's direction, identifying things that bring you pleasure and setting goals. The exercise below will help you focus on specific directions for your life.

EXERCISE ───────────────────────────────

Taking Responsibility for My Life

In your journal spend some time answering the question, "If time and money were no problem, what would I like to do with my life?" Be as imaginative and detailed as possible. Then, because we do live in a world of limitations, think about how you could fulfill your goal realistically. Write down those plans.

For example, if your first statement was, "I'd go live in the South of France and paint," you might then say more realistically, "Next year I'll take a three-week vacation in France, including a week in the South of France to do nothing but paint." Then ask yourself, "How will I accomplish this?" You might reply, "I'll save a hundred dollars per month for the cost of the trip. I'll visit a travel agent and check out air fares and cost of accommodations. I'll also investigate a house exchange with someone in France, or the possibility of staying with a family there for a week. I'll take a course in Impressionist painting at the local college, which will help me to understand how the Impressionists used light in their paintings."

Planning your future is a three-step process:

1. Define your dream (your map).
2. Bring your dream to realistic proportions (your goal).
3. Make definite plans to accomplish your goal (your pathway).

You can work this process again and again as you identify your dreams, set goals, make plans, and implement them. Each time, you assume greater responsibility for your personal fulfillment, which leads you to a satisfying and meaningful life.

You might say that you have always enjoyed books and programs with medical settings and secretly harbored a desire to work in a hospital (your map). You decide to pursue a career as a physical therapy assistant, helping people recover from accidents and illness (your goal). You locate a training program at your local hospital, register, pay the fees, and buy the uniform for clinical classes where you actually work with patients. You also make arrangements for your child to go to a neighbor's house after school on Tuesdays and Thursdays when you have a late class (your pathway).

At 68, Elizabeth found this plan helpful as she struggled to find meaning in a difficult lifestyle imposed by her husband's illness. Committed by her sense of responsibility, overwhelmed by the demands of his illness and her celibacy, and despairing of ever being happy in her marriage again, she worked hard to give old dreams new life.

Elizabeth and Peter had an up-and-down relationship during the first 15 years of their marriage. Sex took its cue from the overall relationship and was sometimes enjoyable and sometimes not. Then, in his fifties, Peter had two major heart attacks. The doctor cautioned him to be careful of exerting himself, and Peter interpreted that to mean that sex was out. In his fear he became a cardiac cripple. "Even when he had an erection he would turn around and walk away from me, which was incredibly painful," Elizabeth said.

Tragedy struck again when Peter was diagnosed with cancer, further tightening the bonds of duty for Elizabeth, who now knew she was in the marriage to the end.

She could not persuade Peter to talk about any of this with her, and at home a thick wall of silence settled between them. Friends, family, and co-workers never knew the anguish she went through. On the surface they maintained the veneer of a devoted couple, calling each other by pet names and treating each other with consideration. "I lived this charade, but underneath I felt tremendous anger; I also felt forced by duty and guilt to stay, because Peter would not be able to live alone financially, and especially not physically." During those years her deep faith in God sustained her.

When Elizabeth did this exercise and looked at her dreams, she realized she'd always wanted to be a ballet dancer. Appreciating that this was not feasible today, she laid out a plan for ways to fill her life with the one thing that had always brought her joy, dancing (her map). She enrolled in ballroom dance classes at the community center (her pathway) and in time became a first-class dancer (her goal). She assumed the responsibility of bringing joy and meaning into her life to counterbalance the intense demands made on her by her husband's illness. Elizabeth was thrilled when she entered and won some regional dance competitions. There were other benefits, Elizabeth explained. "The physical workout of dancing was wonderful for me. It diverted my mind, lifted my spirits, and dancing helped fulfill my need for being held and touched."

Her success on the dance floor gave Elizabeth a sense of mastery and accomplishment she'd never felt before and enhanced her self-esteem. Having no children of her own, she reached out and became close to a family in the neighborhood whose children treated her as another loving grandparent, and she developed good female friends at work.

Peter died shortly after Elizabeth shared her story with us, and when we last talked with her she was again defining her pleasures and charting a course for her future.

Is There Life After Celibacy?

There certainly is life after celibacy! There is much more to life than simply tolerating your lot. Your life can be free of the worry and stress inherent in an unhappy celibate marrriage. If you come to terms with a celibate lifestyle and adopt an attitude of serenity toward your marriage, you may find that:

> much of the negative baggage of your marriage falls away, as it did for Beth and Joel
>
> though no longer a sexual partner, your spouse may not be an enemy either; he may be a good friend, as Jeff was to Marcy
>
> there are strengths in the relationship that you can build on, as Victoria recognized
>
> you are your own person, in charge of your own life, as Kay and Lee discovered
>
> you have renewed energy to explore new opportunities, as Alicia and Elizabeth did
>
> you are stronger than you imagined you were, as every woman in this chapter learned

Perhaps, for the first time in years, your attitudes, hopes, and dreams are creatively centered on yourself. You are the focus of your life. As you work toward re-creating your happiness, sharing with other celibate wives can bring friendship, encouragement, and acceptance as you learn how other women have improved their lives. In our final chapter we will introduce you to a celibate wives support group. We'll allow the women themselves to tell you about the importance of their relationships with one another and how the group helped change their lives.

CHAPTER 8

REACHING OUT

✳ CAMILLA

Talking with other celibate wives makes me feel better about myself. I'm not alone anymore. I learn from what you say, and you've all become important to me.

✳ KAY

I can't believe I'm talking about sex and masturbation. I'm older than the rest of you and I've never talked like this before—it's wonderful to be able to open up like this.

✳ MARIE

I feel 10 pounds lighter now that I'm not carrying the "big secret" anymore. To be able to talk about Dom's abuse and our celibate marriage has been a real blessing.

✳ LINDA

I'm struggling with the decision to leave and I'm terrified to be on my own. Listening to everyone else helps me put my own life into perspective.

If you are still uneasy about your decision to stay or leave your celibate marriage, or if you are terrified of being on your own, finding a friendly forum in which to share your feelings will help you calm your fears and realistically plan for your future. Most celibate wives struggle alone with their celibacy, feeling as if there were a glass wall separating them from other women, whom they assume have normal sexual marriages. They feel too embarrassed to talk about this issue even with their closest friends.

Many women we interviewed expressed relief that they could finally talk with someone about their celibacy and take comfort just knowing they were not alone. This inspired us to organize what we believe to be the first celibate wives self-help group.

We strongly urge you either to find someone to organize a celibate wives self-help group for you, or do it yourself. Your church, community center, women's center, or YWCA might be willing to help you get a group started. If you choose to organize a group yourself, it is not as difficult as you might imagine. In this chapter we will explain how to organize such a group. We'll take the mystery out of the group process by showing you how to facilitate (lead) the group yourself. We will give you the knowledge and tools to create a safe, confidential environment of trust and emotional security for all participants. In doing so we will share some meaningful moments that took place in our celibate wives group.

You may feel that such a group is not for you. You may say, "I don't want to sit around and listen to everyone else's sad stories. I'm already down, and that would make me more depressed." We suggest, try it—even for a few weeks. You just might find that in becoming a part of a celibate wives group you have given yourself a gift. In this supportive setting you can come to grips with the reality of your situation, reevaluate your life, and find support and encouragement for the changes you need to make to create a more fulfilling lifestyle. Often, sharing long-buried secrets will bond you with other members.

A group experience can be informative and meaningful— informative because of the wider perspective you can gain from other members' experiences, and meaningful because you discover you are not alone and are enriched by contact with like-minded souls. The group setting offers an opportunity for women to talk openly about their feelings without fear of being rejected, criticized, or laughed at. Sharing in the group is helpful in a practical sense—Gail said, "Being in this group has helped me to sort things out and moved me closer to making major decisions about my life"—and emotionally satisfying, as when Linda told the group, "I know I am not alone. I know I'm not to blame for the lack of sex in my marriage. I realize now that this happens in many marriages." Camilla agreed. "I've felt more alive and hopeful knowing there are alternatives and seeing what you've all done with your lives." You can gain strength, courage, and hope knowing that other women struggle with the same problems you do.

Being in a group can help you decide whether you should stay or leave your celibate marriage. For example, as you listen to members, it may be that some women have fairly companionable marriages while others live in strife-ridden relationships, and these are powerful considerations in making their decision. As Kay talked about the years during which she tolerated Hugh's verbal abuse, Gail recognized her own life. "That's me," she exclaimed. "There's no way I'm going to live like this indefinitely." Linda, on the other hand, recounted the positive aspects of her life with Carl. "Except for the anger and frustration I feel about his lack of interest in sex, he treats me very well and I have a lot of control over my life. I go to college and I buy what I want with no questions asked."

Marie was reinforced in her decision to ask Dom to leave when Gail shared her plans for rebuilding her life as a single parent. Gail said, "I've been telling friends that I am going to leave Marc and asking them to help me find a job. I've calculated what my costs will be, and I've discussed leaving with the kids and explained our finances, so they are prepared for the belt-tightening." Several meetings later, Marie turned to Gail and said, "Listening to your plans gave me the courage to talk to my uncle about working in his business, and he's agreed to hire me. I've been scared to tell the kids anything, but I sat down with them and explained that Daddy and I are separating and they seemed as relieved as I am that the fighting will end when Daddy leaves."

ASSEMBLING THE GROUP

The ideal size for a group is from 7 to 10 women. This will allow for those times when some of the members might be unable to attend, leaving enough participants for a meaningful discussion. Here are some suggestions for contacting celibate wives.

1. Place an ad in the local personal column of your newspaper or in an alternative or New Age paper, if your community has one. Such an ad might read:
   WOMEN: Have you or your husband said "No" to sex? Are you living in a celibate marriage? You are not alone. Self-help

203

group forming for support and friendship. Call or contact: (use your first name only and a phone number, or rent a box at a post office or a mailbox center).

You may need to run the ad several times. Women may be hesitant about responding when they first read it, for it takes time to absorb a new idea. They may need time to consider if this might be right for them.

2. Prepare a one-sheet flyer based on the information in the ad and place it in a women's center, church, or YWCA. Be sure to include a phone number or address where interested women can contact you.

3. Place a notice in the bookstore where you bought your copy of *Celibate Wives*. Explain to the staff that you are trying to form a celibate wives self-help group.

4. Contact your local YWCA, adult education program, or community school to see if they would sponsor such a group and advertise it in their bulletin; if you prefer, you might ask them if they could interest a local counselor in leading such a group.

THE INTRODUCTORY MEETING

When enough women are interested, the initial, "Hello, I am . . ." meeting should be informal, perhaps over coffee and dessert. Choose a neutral environment for your meetings, perhaps a church basement, clubhouse, or community center meeting room. Find a place where phones will not ring, family will not intrude, and you are away from the normal pressures of daily life. Comfortable chairs set in a circle help people relax. This first meeting should include introductions and the sharing of structural and group interaction guidelines.

Name tags, with first names only, should be used at the first meeting. Ask members to introduce themselves and to tell everyone who they are and why they came to the group. Participants will probably be nervous. Lead off by introducing yourself and telling the group why you invited them to gather.

If you start by saying, "I'm Mary. I have three children and I am glad you are here," you are setting a superficial tone, and others will take a cue from you. You will set an open, caring tone if you begin with an honest sharing of your concerns. For example: "I'm Mary and I'm a celibate wife. I want very much to meet other women who share my concerns, talk about my life, and hear how you are handling your lives. I've lived here for ten years now and I like it. I've been married for what seems like forever, but it's only twelve years. I've been celibate for the last two years and am trying to decide how to cope with this, if I can live with it or need to think about getting out, which is tough with three kids." Talk for between two and five minutes, no longer. In being open you can create an atmosphere in which members can relax and are willing to share their lives.

Establish a time frame for introductions. For example, if there are 10 women and you allow 5 minutes for each to speak, you are using 50 minutes for introductions. Don't be anxious if some women do not talk for the whole five minutes. Just relax, and when everyone has introduced herself, go on with the business of the meeting, allowing time for questions. Light refreshments at the end of the meeting will provide the opportunity for women to chat with one another. (For all following meetings, in order to time one another we have found it helpful to have the member to the left of the speaker hold a watch. When five minutes are up, or the woman finishes speaking, the watch-holder simply passes the watch to the speaker. That woman then times the person to her right, and so on.)

At our first group meeting Kay said, "I am incredibly nervous being here. I'm basically shy and I've never discussed sex or celibacy with anyone. I'm an artist and I own a gallery. I'm also a grandmother, and that's been a real blessing."

This was followed by Gail's disclosure of surprise: "I thought no one else was living without sex in marriage. It seemed freaky to me. I thought I was alone with this problem, so I'm here because I need to talk about this and to know what other people are doing."

At that initial meeting, Roxanne told us, "I'm glad to be here. I've always wanted people to talk to about this problem. My husband and I used to have great sex, and sex is still very important to me, but not with him. My husband is the great couch potato, watching TV every moment he's home. He's rude and crude and he's gotten fat, all of which turn me off."

It did not take long for us all to start relaxing. We had a great deal we wanted to share and were eager to hear what other women had to say.

At later meetings, as facilitator, begin by saying, "Shall we start?" or, "Would someone like to begin?" This will encourage others and you will not find yourself always taking the lead.

GROUP GUIDELINES

Everyone needs to have a clear idea of the basic guidelines that control the business of the group.

1. Agree on a time, day, place, and number of weeks you will meet. (We suggest that meetings last two hours.)
2. Agree to start and stop on time.
3. Agree to take group breaks. People slipping out periodically can interrupt the flow and insult the person speaking.
4. Establish a system for contacting members in an emergency.
5. Set smoking rules if there are any smokers in the group.

6. Agree to keep everything said in the group confidential. Members must pledge not to discuss with others anything heard in the group. We cannot stress enough the importance of each woman feeling certain that her trust will not be betrayed by another member.

Choosing Topics and Taking Turns

1. All group members can participate in generating discussion topics. Ask members to write on slips of paper issues of concern to them. Place the slips in a container. At the end of each session, one slip is pulled from the container; that becomes the topic for the following week. This allows everyone a chance to think about the issue before the next meeting. Topics might include: what it feels like to be a celibate wife, coping with depression, dealing with anger, loneliness, self-blame, and expectations about marriage and sex.

2. Limit each meeting to two rounds of talking, with everyone having a turn to speak for not more than five minutes each time. The first time around, limit your discussion to the topic that has been chosen. In the second round, you might wish to elaborate on the topic. The second round of talk is more casual. As you interact, perhaps you will ask one another for clarification or express agreement.

3. Occasionally a member may need time to gather her thoughts. If a member chooses to let her turn pass, allow her the opportunity to speak at the end of that round. We have found that once everyone feels comfortable in the group, few (if any) let the opportunity to share their experiences pass by.

4. If the conversation is becoming general or drifting into

banalities, a gentle reminder will help the group to refocus: "I feel we are getting off the topic."

Marie is an example of a woman who needed time to feel comfortable before talking. Introducing herself she said, "I have two daughters. I'm scared to be here. I won't talk much right now." But most of the women were eager to talk about themselves and to share, at last, their own experiences and hear what other women were thinking and feeling.

Roxanne was very open from the first meeting. "I am delighted to be here. I'm brimming over with things I want to talk about. I'm really conflicted because sex is important to me and this is my third marriage, so it's hard for me to leave. I worry there must be something wrong with me for wanting out of yet another marriage. I feel very frustrated. I work full time, so I stay busy, and besides my normal routine, it helps me to work out—aerobics several days a week. I've been putting off serious decision-making and I'm hoping I can talk about all of this with you."

Strategies for Successful Communication

Strategies for communication that should become routine in your group include:

Speaking personally with "I" messages
Listening attentively to others
Accepting others without judgment, advice, or criticism
Being empathetic by trying to put yourself in the speaker's shoes

"I" Messages. An "I" message starts with taking responsibility for yourself by saying, "I feel," or "I think." This is not always

easy. Many of us are accustomed to generalizing and deperson-alizing our statements by saying "you think" or "you feel." This implies that you know how another person feels. All you really know is how *you* feel or think. As you interact, allow members to gently remind one another by saying "I" when someone uses the more comfortable "you." By the second or third meeting everyone should be aware of "I" messages and be more careful when sharing thoughts and feelings.

At a later session, Marie, who was now very comfortable expressing her feelings, said, "You know, you feel rotten, you feel devastated." When we reminded her to change the "you" to "I" she did so, smiling as she continued. "I'm sorry. Of course it's 'I.' I felt devastated being celibate. My self-confidence hit rock bottom. I didn't want to see people—it affected my social life because I felt that anyone seeing us together could tell."

Listening. Listening is difficult because when others speak, you are often busily thinking of how you will respond. Con-versely, how many times in the course of normal social conver-sation have you felt unheard and misunderstood by the person you were speaking to? Listening requires your full attention. When you hear what others are saying you can visualize possi-bilities for your own life. You say to yourself, "Gee, if that worked for her, maybe it would work for me too." You can also learn from other women's mistakes. When Joan told of the stress and anxiety surrounding an affair she had had, Linda admitted she had been considering an affair and didn't think she could cope with that kind of stress.

Guarantee each member of the group uninterrupted time to share her thoughts and feelings. It is important that everyone feels comfortable expressing her feelings without anyone inter-rupting, arguing, criticizing, or telling her what to do. You give someone a gift when you offer your undivided attention, without judgment or advice.

This undivided attention was very obvious one evening when we were talking about depression. Women leaned forward, listening intently to one another, and it was clear that everyone felt she had been deeply traumatized at some point by depression. Gail told us, "I didn't know why I was so immobilized. It was as if my brain and my body barely functioned, and I couldn't do anything big where I had to commit myself for more than a couple of days. I wasn't up to any more than that. I moved like an automaton, and when I glimpsed myself in a mirror my eyes had a glazed look that shocked me. I buried my feelings, made superficial small talk, and didn't tell anyone how I really felt."

Roxanne responded, "I had a period of depression which was omnipresent and dominated my entire waking hours, and I wasn't strong enough to overcome it. I prided myself on being a very strong person, but that time I couldn't handle it alone and I ended up going to counseling for help."

Camilla offered her method for coping with depression: "I deal with depression by staying very busy. I don't look depressed even when I'm in the pits. I move and do things swiftly—many things—all the time, like a merry-go-round, spinning faster and faster. People think of depression as totally debilitating, but I don't stop going. I'm on the go so much, even my closest friend doesn't recognize that I'm depressed."

Marie had the opposite reaction to depression. "Depression shows all over me. My face sags, my body feels dragged down, and anyone seeing me just knows something is very wrong with me. I can't stand having it bottled up inside of me and I have to talk about it too, but people really don't want to hear about how depressed you are day after day. Sometimes if I'd meet a stranger, like on a plane or in the beauty parlor, I'd find myself telling that person my life story and how bad I feel, and it's a relief to know I'll never see that person again."

Acceptance. Acceptance means taking each member for who she is, not asking her to be like yourself. This is a major goal of the group. When you accept someone, you accept her feelings and thoughts as valid for her, and you give each member the right to freely and comfortably express her deepest fears and hopes in a safe environment of trust.

After a number of meetings of our group, the topic drawn from the box one evening was sexual fantasies, dreams, and masturbation. By this time we members felt very comfortable with one another and found it easy to talk about such intimate concerns. Linda admitted, "I've dreamed I'm with this exciting guy. I go through the turned-on stage, but I don't reach orgasm. That's frustrating."

This struck a chord with Camilla. "I dream too, and in my dreams there's lots of foreplay, followed by wonderfully fulfilling intercourse. Sometimes I wake up groaning with pleasure. It upsets me though—reminds me of what I'm missing."

Kay laughed. "Well, you got me so curious about masturbating, I went home and tried it. Don't forget, I never have had an orgasm at all. It seemed like a lot of work for the result, and I decided I'd rather not do it again. Why stir up something that's been dead for so many years?"

Empathy. Empathy means putting yourself into the other woman's shoes, feeling her feelings and offering understanding. Empathy means taking time to ask yourself, "If I were Gail or Linda, how would I be feeling?" By the fourth week our celibate wives had begun to genuinely care for one another. Gail articulated everyone's feelings by saying. "I'm surprised at how many times I think about you all during the week." Feeling free to share her deepest worries, she continued, "I have such a poor self-image I'm not able to think of having a life of my own. I feel dependent and frightened of my husband's overall controlling behavior. He treats me as though I am incompetent, and I feel that way."

Gail's comments touched a chord in Kay, who reached out to touch Gail's hand. Kay said, "I felt inadequate—that I couldn't do anything right. Hugh used to yell at me that I was stupid. After I had therapy I realized that his words were just that, words, and I didn't have to accept them, as I had been, as gospel."

Linda felt completely understood when she verbalized her fear and pain about leaving her marriage. "I have so many doubts. I don't want to leave my marriage. I can't support myself. How could I ever afford to finish my education? I don't think I will ever form another relationship, and I don't want to be alone for the rest of my life. So my dilemma is, if I leave because I'm celibate, what's going to happen to me? I'm almost 50 and I'm overweight. Who'd want me?"

It was clear, by the concerned and caring expressions on the faces of other members and the nodding of heads, that many of us understood Linda's pain and fear.

Camilla was particularly sensitive to Linda's feelings. "I also feel very afraid of having to go it alone. I'm not sure I can make it on my own out there. Like you, I'm trying to get my degree and it seems years away. Why don't you call me and let's see if together we can't generate some activity to make us both feel better?" This was the beginning of what has become a close friendship.

We hope that reading this chapter, seeing how these women made choices and gained a sense of power interacting with one another, has given you the courage to start your own celibate wives self-help group. Such a group is one more step along the way as you make choices and take chances. Don't put it off, begin to plan today. In doing so you can help yourself and the other women in your group to become prime movers in your own lives, as you focus your energy and creativity on getting from where you are to where you want to be.

Whether you decide upon a group, private therapy, or talking with someone you trust and respect, our hearts and hope for good fortune go with you. Have faith and confidence in yourself. We trust that you will draw on the power within you on your journey of self-exploration and make wise decisions as you pave the way to your happier, brighter future.

EPILOGUE

AND NOW FAREWELL

Writing this book has been a challenge, a grand adventure, and a life-changing event. New career paths opened for us, and we met interesting and wonderful people. Drawing on latent talents, we took risks that set our dreams into action.

Many years ago, Joan asked her father how she could find happiness. His reply seemed illusive to a 20-year-old. "Happiness," he said, "is not a goal in itself. It is found along the way, and especially in doing something you love."

She says today, "My wise father was right. The writing of *Celibate Wives* has been an act of love. The process has given meaning and fulfillment to my life, and I have indeed found happiness along the way."

Diana, struggling to leave her marriage, lived the process chapter by chapter as the book was being written. "I grieved what might have been in my marriage and accepted that it was not possible to rekindle sex, nor to change my husband, and I accepted responsibility for building a good life for myself."

David Viscott's quote from chapter six, "Each person must take the risk of creating a life of his own, assembling the best parts of his past and weaving them together into a story that has the most optimistic future," struck a chord deep within Diana. Re-creating her life became a viable possibility. She began to review her life and pull out those things that had brought her the most happiness. Then she took those elements and crafted them into a believable future for herself in terms of where to live, what areas of counseling and writing she wanted to pursue, and what activities would bring her the greatest satisfaction.

"I realized that I could take the best parts of my life and create a future. Since this fell into place I have a sense of excitement and adventure about my future instead of dread. This vision of my life feels real and it fits. I am looking forward to the challenges and opportunities the next few years will bring."

We hope that you will solve your celibacy problem in ways that bring you satisfaction and happiness. As you proceed, look for these changes that will characterize your personal transformation:

You act spontaneously, and with joy, and your behavior will not be based on outdated, mistaken beliefs and fears.

You are more accepting of yourself and your husband as well as other people.

You no longer need to criticize or judge others, and you avoid conflict.

You no longer allow anxiety and worry to overwhelm you or control your life.

You feel more connected with others, and have a deeper sense of knowing that all is well.

You believe in yourself and feel that the world around you is filled with possibilities.

You are re-creating a future for yourself.

Grasp the brass ring, that solid symbol of getting what you want. The world is indeed filled with alternatives and possibilities on which you can build a good and happy life.

APPENDIX

HOW TO FIND
A THERAPIST

The first step, if you have health insurance, is to check exactly what kind of psychological coverage you have, if any. Most policies cover treatment by psychiatrists and psychologists. Many highly skilled master's-level therapists work in conjunction with Ph.D's and M.D.'s so that their treatment can be covered by insurance.

Many people ask someone they know and respect for a referral to a therapist, or you might ask your doctor or minister. Mental health centers and Catholic and Jewish family services usually have a sliding-fee scale in which payment is based on income. The United Way often funds mental health programs to which they can refer you.

If your celibacy causes you great anger or depression, or you are torn by indecision whether to stay in or leave your marriage, tell a potential therapist exactly what your concerns are and ask how much experience she or he has had working with people on these issues. Severe depression and suicidal thoughts require immediate attention, so you will need to assert yourself. Insist, if necessary, that you be seen by the therapist within the next few days. Be open about how depressed you are and how you need help quickly.

If you have decided to try to fix the sex in your marriage, you need to see a qualified sex therapist. Treatment should include psychological as well as specific sex therapy. For names of certified sex therapists, call these numbers and ask for a referral in your area.

American Association of Sex Education, Counseling and Therapy, 1-312-644-0528

American Board of Sexology, 1-202-462-2122

If your focus is on leaving your marriage, you want to find a therapist who can work with you in a problem-solving manner with practical suggestions to help you through this difficult period. Good therapy will help you to understand what went wrong in your marriage and why you chose the husband you did: hopefully, this insight will keep you from making the same mistake again.

A divorce or separation support group may also be helpful. Your therapist can probably refer you to one or may have put such a group together. Your local newspaper may list support groups, or check with your mental health center, local churches, or women's center.

Should staying in the marriage be your choice, you will have to find a therapist who is comfortable working with you and the decision you have made, who will not automatically say, "Anyone living in a celibate marriage must get out." Many therapists we talked with told us that about 20 percent of their clients are living in celibate marriages. Some are working to get out, while others are dealing with staying. You need to ask the therapist if she or he has worked with clients who are living in your situation.

Therapy doesn't always feel good. There may be times when your therapist pushes you to deal with issues that upset you, but you should not feel upset after all or most of your sessions. After the initial few sessions, you should trust your therapist, feel that she or he has your best interests at heart and keeps your therapy on a strictly professional basis. It is counterproductive for your therapist to make you a part of her or his personal, private life or to become a part of yours. You should not stand in awe of your therapist. Be a knowledgeable consumer by asking questions about the therapist's training, what the goals will be for your therapy, and what her or his experience has been in dealing with celibate marriages. You may find that you need to interview several potential therapists before you find one with whom you feel comfortable enough to discuss the most intimate aspects of your life. Let each therapist know that you will be talking with several others before making a decision.

We have found it most helpful to contract with the therapist for a certain number of weeks or months of therapy. A time frame often moves the work along more rapidly. At the end of this period, if you both agree that you should continue, you can contract for another period of time.

Therapy offers deeper self-understanding, emotional support, and help with important decision-making. It might be the greatest gift you can give yourself. Additional resources are included following the bibliography and suggested readings.

BIBLIOGRAPHY

Beattie, Melody. *Codependent No More*. New York: Harper/Hazelden, 1987.

Brown, Gabrielle. *The New Celibacy*. New York: McGraw-Hill, 1980.

Engel, Beverly. *The Emotionally Abused Woman*. Los Angeles: Lowell House, 1990.

Kaplan, Helen Singer, M.D. *Disorders of Sexual Desire*. New York: Simon & Schuster, 1979.

———. "Why Did My Husband Turn Me Off?" *Redbook*, December 1986.

Kline, Nathan S. *From Glad to Sad*. New York: Ballantine, 1987.

Knopf, Jennifer, M.D., and Michael Seiler, M.D. *ISD, Inhibited Sexual Desire*. New York: William Morrow and Co., 1990.

Landers, Ann. "Sex and Marriage." *Palm Beach Post*, June 26, 1990.

Lederer, William J., and Don D. Jackson, M.D. *The Mirages of Marriage*. New York: W. W. Norton and Co., 1968.

Leman, Kevin, M.D., and Randy Carlson. *Unlocking the Secrets of Your Childhood Memories*. Nashville: Thomas Nelson Publishers, 1989.

Masters, William H., and Virginia E. Johnson. *Human Sexual Inadequacy*. Boston: Little Brown and Co., 1970.

Masters, William H., and Virginia E. Johnson. *Human Sexuality*. 3rd Ed., Scott Forsman Co., Glenview, IL, 1988.

Pittman, Frank. *Private Lies: Infidelity and the Betrayal of Intimacy*. New York: W. W. Norton and Co., 1989.

Rubin, Theodore I., M.D. *The Angry Book*. New York: Macmillan, 1969.

Tatelbaum, Judith. *The Courage to Grieve*. New York: Harper & Row, 1980.

Tavris, Carol. *Anger, The Misunderstood Emotion*. New York: Simon & Schuster, 1982.

Viscott, David, M.D. *Risking*. New York: Simon & Schuster, 1977.

SUGGESTED READINGS

CHIILDHOOD SEXUAL ABUSE

Bass, Ellen, and Laura Davis. *The Courage to Heal: A Guide for Women Survivors of Child Sexual Abuse*. New York: Harper & Row, 1988.

Engel, Beverly. *The Right to Innocence: Healing the Tragedy of Childhood Sexual Abuse*. Los Angeles: Jeremy Tarcher, 1976.

CODEPENDENCE

Covington, Stephanie, and Liana Beckett. *Leaving the Enchanted Forest*. San Francisco: Harper & Row, 1989.

Hay, Louise L. *You Can Heal Yourself*. Santa Monica, CA: Hay House, 1984.

Schaef, Anne Wilson. *Co-Dependence: Misunderstood—Mistreated*. San Francisco: Harper & Row, 1986.

DEPRESSION

Gold, Mark S., M.D. *The Good News About Depression. New York:* Bantam Books, 1986.

Greist, John H., M.D.; James W. Jefferson, M.D; and Isaac M. Marks, M.D. *Depression and Its Treatment*. New York: Warner Books, 1984.

DIVORCE

Robertson, Christina. *A Woman's Guide to Divorce and Decision Making: A Supportive Workbook for Women Facing the Process of Divorce*. New York: Fireside, Simon & Schuster, 1989.

Trafford, Abigail. *Crazy Time: Surviving Divorce*. New York: Bantam Books, 1982.

RELATIONSHIPS

Lernet, Harriet Goldhor. *The Dance of Intimacy*. New York: Harper & Row, 1989.

Norwood, Robin. *Women Who Love Too Much*. New York: Pocket Books, 1986.

SELF-DISCOVERY

Bradshaw, John. *On the Family: A Revolutionary Way of Self-Discovery*. Deerfield Beach, FL: Health Communications, 1988.

Bridges, William. *Transitions: Making Sense of Life's Changes*. Menlo Park, CA: Addison-Wesley, 1980.

Fritz, Robert. *The Path of Least Resistance*. New York: Fawcett Columbine, 1984.

Koller, Alice. *An Unknown Woman: A Journey of Self-Discovery*. New York: Bantam, 1983.

Mornwell, Pierre, M.D. *Passive Men—Wild Women*. New York: Ballantine Books, 1980.

Schaef, Anne Wilson. *Women's Reality: An Emerging Female System in a White Male Society*. New York: Harper & Row, 1981.

SELF-ESTEEM

Branden, Nathaniel. *Honoring the Self: The Psychology of Confidence and Respect*. New York: Bantam Books, 1983.

Jeffers, Susan. *Feel the Fear and Do It Anyway*. New York: Fawcett Columbine, 1988.

Sanford, Linda Tschirhart, and Mary Ellen Donovan. *Women and Self-Esteem*. New York: Viking Penguin, 1985.

SEXUALITY

Barbach, Lonnie. *For Each Other: Sharing Sexual Intimacy*. New York: Signet, 1984.

———. *For Yourself: The Fulfillment of Female Sexuality*. New York: Anchor Books, Doubleday Dell, 1975.

Helmering, Doris Wild. *Husbands, Wives and Sex*. Holbrook, MA: Bob Adams Inc., 1990.

Shotz, Fred. *The Better Sex Video Series,* Counseling Associates, 2699 Stirling Road, Suite A–304, Fort Lauderdale, FL 33312.

Yaffe, Maurice; Elizabeth Fenwick; and Raymond Rosen. *Sexual Happiness for Women, a Practical Approach*. New York: Henry Holt and Co., 1986.

RESOURCES

WHERE TO TURN FOR HELP

National Domestic Violence Hotline
1-800-333-7233

Centers for Disease Control National Clearing House on AIDS
1-800-458-5231

National HIV and AIDS Information Service
1-800-342-2437

Co-Dependents Anonymous
(CODA)
602-277-7991

VOICES (Victims of Incest
Can Emerge Survivors) in Action, Inc.
313-327-1500

Parents overwhelmed by parental responsibility can call: Childhelp USA
818-347-7280

Parents who have sexually abused a child can call: Parents United
408-280-5055

or

Parents Anonymous National Hotline
1-800-775-1134
1-800-352-0386

INDEX

231